My Altered Self

To Zainey,
God's Blessing
Sue Foster

Praise For My Altered Self

My Altered Self is an inspiration. Thanks Sue, for doing the work—finding the truth about what happened to you, seeking healing, and ending up in joy.

—Dr. James G. Friesen, PhD
Psychologist and Minister
Pioneer in treatment of Multiple
Personality Dissociative Disorders
Author of best-selling *Uncovering the Mystery of MPD*

When looking over Sue Liston's book *My Altered Self*, I am reminded of so many times when Sue was confronted with obstacles on every side. Instead of falling under them, she rose up and confronted the enemy face to face, struggling within and without to fight a battle that could have overwhelmed her, having the confidence from that deep place within where God lives that she could win. This book will help others to see and understand ever more clearly a subject that has been so deeply hidden by the darkness itself.

—Dr. Marilyn Marshall PhD
Marriage and Family Therapist,
Specializing in MPD/DID and PTSD

When Sue Liston first told me she wanted to write a book about her life with Dissociative Identity Disorder, I asked what her purpose would be. Without hesitation, she replied, 'I want people to know there is a spiritual battle between good and evil—and it is real. I also want them to know that there is hope for everyone caught up in such a battle.' Sue has accomplished this with her book *My Altered Self*. As a therapist, I appreciate Sue's willingness to share her own journey of inner turmoil, struggle, and pain as well as her fearless determination to reach out with the truth that God is our Redeemer and his love and grace is for everyone.

—Margie Amador-Alvarado, MA, CPC
Psychotherapist
CEO Amador De Alvarado Counseling & Consulting

In *My Altered Self*, Sue Liston has written a gripping personal narrative that begins with a severely dysfunctional family, followed by a resulting personality disorder, ending with a faith journey and professional counseling. The author writes of her journey with clarity and sincerity. You will find this book inspiring, informative, and even disturbing with some questions still unanswered.

—Dr. Arthur Seamans
Emeritus Professor of Literature
Point Loma Nazarene University

What an encouragement this book is for anyone who has ever felt hopeless, helpless, worthless, or irredeemable. In *My Altered Self*, Sue takes you on her life journey and leads you to the only Person who can radically change your life today and forever, Jesus Christ. Through faith in Jesus, you can overcome your trials and walk in victory right now, today. As you read each chapter, you will see there is joy and hope after heartache and brokenness. Read this book and be changed forever.

–Melinda Kramb
Women's Ministry Leader
San Diego, CA

Sue teaches Bible classes, is a fabulous hostess, parents her daughters with love and commitment, nurtures her devoted husband, and is involved in countless other activities. Yet no one could guess her darkness and despair when repressed multiple personalities periodically take over her life. How Sue not only survives, but thrives is a compelling and moving story. In *My Altered Self,* you will join Sue on a journey through darkness and despair to the light she finds at the end of the tunnel, which is God's redemptive grace and the comfort of God's loving embrace.

—June Green
BS, Sociology

My Altered Self is a fantastic, truly amazing story of our Lord's protection and care, using methods that defy imagination and yet Jesus allowed all to work together for good.

—Linda Biesel
women's Bible study leader
San Diego, CA

My Altered Self

How God's Gift of Multiple Personality Disorder Redeemed my Nightmare Childhood

By Sue Liston

SANL619 Publishing
El Cajon CA

Copyright © 2017
By Sue Liston

SANL619 Publishing

ISBN 978-0-6929479-4-4

contact author at **www.suelistonbks.com**

book and e-book designed and formatted by

www.ebooklistingservices.com

1 3 5 7 9 10 8 6 4 2

Printed in the United States of America

Dedication

I could write an entire book on my husband **Larry Liston**, love of my life and my best friend for over fifty-five years. From the instability of my dysfunctional family, he has brought me happiness, security, and the encouragement to fulfill my talents and potentialities. During my six-year journey of writing this book, he has been the teleological giant who keeps my computer running smoothly.

I dedicate this book as well to:

Our two daughters, **Dena Myers** and **Donna Ryan**, who give me great joy and deep satisfaction. Without their approval in disclosing sensitive family issues in my book, my book wouldn't have been written.

Sandy McNulty, my sister, who has been with me every step of my writing journey, authenticating our past recollections and giving me encouragement to share my story with others.

My many friends who know my story and accept me without judgement. They've given me confidence to share my story to a public audience.

Acknowledgements

I would like to express my gratitude to **Linda Smith**, my creative writing teacher at Grossmont adult school in San Diego. From when I first entered her class as a fledging novice, Linda provided me the tools to finish this book, teaching me how to craft the right words and give shape to its images. Within the friendly environment of her classroom, my writing voice came alive.

Also, I wouldn't be where I am today without my wonderful therapists, **Dr. Marilyn Marshall** and **Margie Alvarado**. Under their skilled knowledge and undying care, each successfully treated my Multiple Personality Disorder by working through and stabilizing my alternate identities.

My editor, **Jeanette Windle**, is an encourager and an expert editor who has cut out, added, and clarified my story to bring about a polished product. I am very grateful to her.

And to my brilliant indie publisher, **Amy Deardon**, who has walked me through the entire publishing process of my book, including its cover design and interior, formatting, etc.

Table of Contents

Introduction
  Victory 1
Chapter One
  Splintered..7
Chapter Two
  The Doorway Opens...15
Chapter Three
  Resilience..25
Chapter Four
  Tenacity...31
Chapter Five
  Survival...41
Chapter Six
  Peace..47
Chapter Seven
  Fear..55
Chapter Eight
  Nature's Soothing Balm.....................................63
Chapter Nine
  Presence..69
Chapter Ten
  Troubled Waters..77
Chapter Eleven
  Recovery...83
Chapter Twelve
  A Tight Grip...91
Chapter Thirteen
  God's Messenger...99
Chapter Fourteen
  Discipline..107
Chapter Fifteen
  Perseverence..115
Chapter Sixteen
  God's Leading..121
Chapter Seventeen
  Patience...129

Chapter Eighteen
    Help..135
Chapter Nineteen
    Divine Guidance...141
Chapter Twenty
    God's Love..145
Chapter Twenty-One
    Strength...151
Chapter Twenty-Two
    Unending Trials..157
Chapter Twenty-Three
    God's Intervention...165
Chapter Twenty-Four
    Evil Thwarted...175
Chapter Twenty-Five
    Our Enemy...183
Chapter Twenty-Six
    Protection...191
Chapter Twenty-Seven
    Salvation...201
Chapter Twenty-Eight
    Restoration...209
Chapter Twenty-Nine
    Indefatigable...215
Chapter Thirty
    Ownership...221
Chapter Thirty-One
    Gifts..227
Chapter Thirty-Two
    Direction...235
Chapter Thirty-Three
    God's Hand...241
Chapter Thirty-Four
    Truth..249
Epilogue
    Future Hope..255

About the Author...258

My Altered Self

INTRODUCTION

VICTORY

Be of good cheer, I have overcome the world.
—John 16:33

I am so blessed! God has gifted me with a wonderful husband and good marriage, two beautiful daughters, grandchildren I adore, a healthy body and sound mind, a life I enjoy, and lots of friends.

I have also been gifted with a more unusual blessing—Multiple Personality Disorder, or Dissociative Identity Disorder, as it is more commonly termed today. Not many people would categorize such as a blessing, and it took me many years to come to terms with my condition or the gift from God it really was. At least two of my counselors have concluded that without MPD, I would have committed suicide by now or ended up permanently in a mental institution.

My life began as very much the fairy-tale American dream. Two attractive, highly-intelligent, successful parents. A prosperous upper-middle-class home. The cliché white

1

clapboard house complete with window boxes, picket fence, and tree-filled back yard. A big sister for playmate. What could be better?

But behind the closed shutters of that American dream house lurked a nightmare. My loving, smart, handsome father was also a crazed, mentally-ill man who rotated in and out of a sanitarium. Overwhelmed with Daddy's problems, along with her own mental and emotional issues, my mother had no love or concern to give to her daughters.

When my extreme emotional pain and shaken security became more than I could handle, God in His infinite mercy and care gave me the gift of dissociation that took my trauma and stored it safely in a mental lockbox. In this lock-box were many rooms containing alternate personalities, or alters, as they are termed, who held and fought the internal battles of my mind. Each was unique, and each was very different from the Sue Liston I was and knew. Some were bad-hearted. Some were good-hearted.

But each worked together to protect my fragile sanity. This enabled me to function normally enough to survive the years of abuse, violence, sexual molestation, and satanic oppression that made up my childhood. Instead of being swallowed up in pain or paralyzed by suffering, I was not even aware that my childhood was cruel or that I was suffering from parental neglect.

God also gifted me with a childhood delight in His creation. The delicate flowers and green trees. Bird songs and rushing water. The small creatures and creepy-crawlies that lived around our home. Sunrises and sunsets. Blue skies. Billowing clouds. Rainbows. These became my escape and sanctuary. However dark and terrifying my home life, they offered assurance that this world also held beauty, light, and hope.

Not that I escaped unscathed. In decades that followed, I endured unexplained depression and anxieties. By then, I'd built a good life for myself with a loving husband and two daughters. Engaging activities and sound relationships filled my time. So I could not understand why I still felt so miserable.

I endured another mental suffering that was even worse. I went to church every Sunday with my husband and his family. I knew the Bible held truth. But I could neither read the Bible nor accept Jesus. Even the mention of Jesus stirred up intense agitation in me.

Still, through all this God was with me. He not only gave me the gift of dissociation so that inner trauma would not overwhelm me, but also divinely brought the right people into my life to offer me counsel and in God's timing lead me to Himself. This includes Christian counselors and ministry leaders who were able to uncover my multiple personality disorder, help me face demonic oppression, and put me on the journey to self-discovery and healing.

I was fifty-three years old when I came face to face with Jesus Christ in a born-again experience that transformed my life. From that day forward, Jesus became my cornerstone, the core of my hope and healing, my Savior who has set me free. And instead of being a dusty book I was afraid to open, the Bible came alive to me as God's inspired Word, given to teach us and guide us into His eternal love.

With Jesus in my heart and life, I could now venture unafraid into the darkness of my past. Which in turn has allowed me to finally put the past behind me and move forward into God's light and life. This does not mean I no longer have MPD. My alters will always be part of my mind and life. But as I have come to peace with them and their role in protecting my mind and emotions, they in turn have found peace and have largely integrated into a Sue Liston who is now whole, healed, and living in a joyous freedom I never would have dreamed possible.

It was also God's guidance that took me to a Christian writer's conference, where I heard the speaker say, "If you've had an unusual or remarkable experience that reveals the glory of God, you need to tell your story."

At the time, I really had no idea why I'd attended that writer's conference in the first place. I wasn't a writer. I didn't even like to write. At my age, it seemed far too late to start.

But God had other plans. His voice came through clearly to me. "Write your story."

"But God, I'm not a writer!" I argued.

His answer was unambiguous. "Write the book."

And so I did. You are holding it in your hands right now. As you read it, I hope that my experiences will be of help and encouragement along your own journey of self-discovery and healing. We live in such a chaotic world. And we face a real fight against a real enemy, Satan, who uses all his evil guiles to ensnare and enslave us.

But we have a God whose power transcends anything the enemy can send against us. He has guaranteed us the ultimate victory through His Son Jesus Christ. Through His Holy Spirit and in His Word, God has also given us the necessary weapons to demolish Satan's strongholds. The assurance and comfort Jesus gave to His disciples shortly before leaving them to endure the cross and return to heaven is still offered today to anyone who will accept it:

> These things I have spoken to you, so that in Me you
> may have peace. In the world you have tribulation,
> but take courage; I have overcome the world
> —John 16:33).

Other Bible versions translate "take courage" as "take heart" or "be of good cheer". Whatever darkness, sorrow, or tribulation your life may hold, Jesus has already won the battle. And He wants you to experience that victory. Why? Because He loves you so much that He was willing to lay down His life for you.

So as you turn the page and step into my own life journey with me, may I encourage you to take heart. Be of good cheer. Gather up your courage to accept His offer. If you do, I can guarantee that you too will find, as I have, God's victory, peace, and healing in the name of our Lord and Savior Jesus Christ.

Chapter One

SPLINTERED

He will not allow your foot to slip; He who keeps you
will not slumber.

—Psalm 121:3

My day began under a clear blue sky in San
Diego, the city where I lived in southern
California. Even pushing seventy years old, I
was still athletic, and by evening, I'd enjoyed a
good game of tennis, followed by catching a movie with my
husband. But as I settled in for the night, darkness swirled
around me, threatening my soul. Outside, the wind howled,
causing tree branches to brush against my bedroom window.

Punching my down pillow into submission, I yanked the
layered covers up to my neck and clamped my eyes shut. To
push back the buried demons gnawing at my inside, I
focused on my garden where flowers in yellows, pinks, and
blues lifted their heads with a sweet fragrance. The thought
curved my mouth into a slight smile as I drifted off to sleep.

I awoke to lightning and thunder that lit up my room and shook my windows. My night's sleep must have been restless as my covers were now twisted tightly around my body. Unwrapping myself, I rubbed my eyes and checked the small clock that sat on my bedside table. It was only five a.m., too early to get up.

I'll go to the restroom and jump back into bed. Staggering out of bed, I noticed that my nightgown was damp and sticking to my body, my hair stringy from perspiration. A glance in the bathroom mirror revealed an ashen face and glassy eyes. *Oh, I look horrible!*

Looking down, I saw bruises on my legs that hadn't been there when I went to sleep. What had happened during the night? I'd clearly been thrashing around while asleep in some sort of mental turmoil. Had I been releasing the buried rage I'd worked so hard to keep tamped down, away from me, away from my family, away from my friends? I needed to keep tight control. To keep a smile painted on my face. Otherwise, I could lose everything I'd worked so hard to maintain.

Rushing back to bed, I drew the covers around me like a cocoon and stayed there another hour, praying for God's protection from the torture chamber of my mind. Gradually, my tight muscles relaxed and reassuring thoughts took over. *God has lifted me up and carried me through the rough periods in my life. He gave me the gift of dissociation so I could survive a terrifying childhood. I've been born again into new life through the saving grace of Jesus, so the demons of my mind have no more power over me. What do I have to worry about?*

When I finally arose, the storm was over. Forcing a brush through disheveled hair, I applied a bronze foundation to my pale features, then checked my appearance in the bathroom mirror. *Not too bad.*

A beautiful carved-wood wall clock struck 6 a.m. as I followed the smell of coffee down the hall into the kitchen. A wave of sadness swept over me. Daddy had bought me that clock. He'd tried so hard to make a good life for himself, but his life had ended tragically. Was I headed down the same suicidal path?

Stop it, Sue. Don't go there!

In the kitchen, I found my iPad and cell phone on the kitchen counter, being charged. There was no one in sight, but a fresh brew of coffee steamed from the coffee pot. I called out, "Larry, where are you?"

"I'm in the den on the computer," my husband called back, "planning our next trip to India."

Rushing into the den, I wrapped my arms around my husband, Larry, and give him a smooch on the cheek. "You do so much for me—making coffee in the morning, plugging in my electronic gadgets. And now you're planning our next trip. I'm so lucky to have you. What a good life we've had together."

"Feeling's mutual."

"Larry, I sure had a weird experience last night. I woke up a wreck."

My husband glanced up from the computer. "What happened?"

"The storm woke me up. But I'm sure it goes beyond that. Though I can't remember anything, I must have had a terrible nightmare, because I woke up all sweaty and snarled in the covers."

"Don't worry. You look great. It was just a dream." Giving me a pat on my shoulder, Larry turned back to his computer.

Not wanting to alarm him, I kept my bruised legs hidden beneath my nightgown as I headed back to the kitchen to pour myself a cup of coffee laced with plenty of milk and sugar. As I sat down at the table, I lifted my nightgown to rub my bruised legs. They hurt. I shuddered. A chill rushed down my spine.

Hunching over, I buried my face in my hands as images of past counseling sessions roiled in my mind. I'd been diagnosed with Dissociative Identity Disorder, previously known as a Multiple Personality Disorder. It was not a condition I'd been consciously aware of. But in the safety net of my therapist's office, personality fragments, called splits or alters, had exposed their individual identities of stored memories and feelings that I myself didn't experience on a conscious level. In fact, each of these alters, or multiple personalities, states vehemently that they are not me.

At the time when these other identities emerge during counseling sessions, I am not aware of them. But once I come back into myself (the host), I can remember clearly each occurrence. One alter that spoke in a foreign guttural voice threw Bibles, ripped a cross off my neck, and caused me to roll on the floor. I left that session drenched in sweat with chipped teeth and painfully tight muscles in my neck.

Other alters adopted the persona of wolves, lions, and snakes, using their strength and power to help fight off approaching danger. Some alters emerged filled with hate and rage, blaming me for their pain and accusing me of not deserving parental support, care, and love. Some denied having any feelings or memories at all, while others dissociated from having a physical body, insisting they were only a spirit.

Counselors have explained that such dissociation protects a child from experiencing overwhelming trauma beyond their ability to cope. But I'd never really understood just what in my past could have triggered such a huge mass of anger, hostility, and strange behavior that was so diametrically opposed to my stable, harmonious everyday life. If my childhood wasn't perfect, I'd always thought it was okay. I'd managed just fine. Appreciated the little things like a roof over my head and food on the table. Kept an upbeat outlook on life.

Straightening my hunched-over body, I picked up the morning's newspaper, which was sitting on the kitchen table. Was my mind still functioning in a rational, intelligent manner, or was I beginning to lose control, slipping into the dark recesses of my inner sanctum, easing into insanity?

I thumbed through the newspaper, looking for the word jumble and Sudoku. After successfully completing both, I put the paper down, satisfied my mind was in working order. But how long could I resume my outward, public demeanor? I needed to look into my past for understanding and healing. My sister might help. I decided to call her.

"Hi Sandy, this is Sue. What cha up to?"

"Not much. What's on your mind?" My only sibling, Sandy was three years older than me. She took after my mother, the Italian side of the family: dark-brown eyes, dark-brown hair, olive skin, and an aquiline nose. I took after my father's Scottish heritage: blond hair, light-golden eyes, a pug nose, and light skin.

I cleared my throat. "As you know, I've been diagnosed as having Dissociative Identity Disorder that is caused from overwhelming trauma. I don't remember any such pain or suffering. But I had a weird experience this morning, woke up drenched in sweat, bruises on my legs. I'm afraid my "other" selves are coming out in my dreams."

"Are you okay now?"

"Yes, but I'm filled with questions. Why did I form a split personality? What happened in my past to warrant such behavior? Have I been satanically abused, molested, or thrown in a closet without food? Maybe you could help me out. Would you be willing to drive by our first house on Dexter Drive in La Mesa? I was only five when we moved. You were eight. Your memories might be clearer than mine."

She breathed in deeply. "Certainly. That's what a sister is for."

The next day I climbed into Sandy's little red Mazda convertible. Our hair blew free in the wind as we zipped down the freeway, made a few sharp turns, and approached the neighborhood where I'd spent my first five years. The little house we'd lived in faced south on the corner.

"Wow, it sure looks old and in disrepair," I commented. "The paint is peeling. The front porch is missing some steps. Even the window screens have holes in them. And the weeds are as tall as me."

"Let's walk down the block and look at our old neighborhood," Sandy suggested.

We did so, our heads whipping back and forth as we checked out the houses, trying to recall who lived there. A fragrance of barbecued meat filled my nostrils. Kids laughed and shrieked in play. There was no reason for the feeling of gloom that swept over me.

Walking back in silence toward Sandy's vehicle, we sat down on the curb in front of the small house where we'd lived. I looked over at Sandy. She was busy picking at something invisible on her jacket, a pained expression on her face. She gave a nod directed across the street.

"See over there? That's where some older neighborhood boys smashed my head against that culvert. A neighbor saw me sitting there, blood running down my head, and walked me home. Another time those same boys forced me into a shed filled with bees and shut the door on me. I went home screaming, covered with welts."

I put my hand across my mouth. "Wow, I never knew about that. If they did that to you, I wonder if they did anything to me."

Sandy's hands clenched together, her eyes narrowed. "I have no idea. But after that, I kept a close watch for them. I was sure glad when we moved."

Turning her head, Sandy stared at our side porch.

"What are you thinking about now?" I asked.

"I remember being tied up on that porch like a dog."

"I don't remember that. How terrible. Why?"

"Mother wanted to keep control of me, not allowing me out of her sight."

"Why?"

Sandy shrugged. "I was adventurous. Wanted to explore. Lost my sense of time."

"That seems like harsh punishment."

We drove back in silence, lost in our thoughts. Before climbing out, I scooted over and gave my sister a hug. She stiffened, yet smiled as she asked, "When am I going to see you again?"

"Soon, I hope," I responded as I climbed out of the convertible. Sandy and I had so much fun now, sharing many common interests like hiking, books, movies, the arts. Yet as a child, I'd considered her a threat to be avoided, someone who might do me harm. Even now, she stiffened when I hugged her. What had happened in that long-ago, forgotten past?

An electronic gate opened onto a steep driveway bordered by melaleuca trees that led up to my own house. A sign announced: *Liston's Lookout.* To my right was our orchard of orange, avocado, peach, plum, and apple trees. The fruit trees were in bloom, their fragrance sweet in my nostrils.

I entered the house. Larry was sitting in his La-Z-Boy chair in the family room, reading the paper. Walking up to him, I cleared my throat. "I had quite a day."

Marking his place with his finger, Larry looked up. "Is this the day you and your sister were going to look at your old house?"

"Yes, we tried to recapture past memories. Sandy came up with a few, but I didn't. Still, I felt nervous and anxious, just being there, looking at our house and trudging through my old neighborhood."

"Maybe you just need to take time to think things over," Larry said. "You always keep yourself so busy, like you're trying to avoid memories of the past."

"You're right," I responded. "Maybe it's time I opened up the sealed compartments of my mind."

Larry picked up the newspaper, discussion over. But just two days later, I shut my bedroom door behind me. With paper and pencil in hand, I sat at my bedroom desk and began the long, arduous process of unraveling my past.

CHAPTER TWO

THE DOORWAY OPENS

The heart of man plans his way, but the Lord establishes his steps.

—Proverbs 16:9

I was a Christmas baby, born December 27, 1941. While to outsiders, it must have seemed that I was born into an ideal life and family, it proved anything but. Both of my parents were considered top prospects for a successful life. My father Edgar had been a popular cheerleader in high school and was voted the most likely to succeed. My mother Jane, was an exceptional student, skipping two grades in school and earning several college scholarships.

The two met at University of California-Berkeley, where as two aspiring intellects they bonded together. My father was studying for his law degree while my mother was a member of the esteemed Phi Beta Kappa Society. She also earned the title of women's tennis champion for the college and eventually graduated with a degree in economics.

Edgar and Jane married shortly after graduation in 1932 with high expectations of a prosperous future. They moved to La Mesa, CA, which was my father's home town. There they settled into a house with blue shutters, white clapboard sidings, and window boxes of geraniums. In the middle of the front lawn, a weeping willow drooped its branches gracefully. A Cecil Brunner climbing rose bloomed along the fence. The backyard was filled with fruit trees just right for children to climb.

With the ingredients of a successful home in place, Edgar set out to establish his law practice. La Mesa is less than twenty miles from San Diego. Locating a vacant office in downtown San Diego overlooking the bay, he formed a partnership with a friend from law school. My father was outgoing and gregarious, which attracted clients. In contrast, his partner was well-organized, keeping everything in order. These complementary abilities contributed to building a very successful practice, specializing in corporate law.

Meanwhile, my mother, Jane, became a stay-at-home housewife, looking forward to raising a family. Six years passed before my older sister Sandra Katheryn—or Sandy, as everyone called her—was born in 1938. I arrived three years later and was given the name Sue Jean. We were now the stereotypical two-parent, two-child American family living in the stereotypical American dream house, complete with picket fence and garden.

But behind closed shutters, our American dream house contained a growing black cloud of despair. My loving father often morphed into a very different man than my mother had known in college and married. In time, we would discover that he had a bipolar dysfunction, a mental disorder that was characterized by extreme shifts in mood from severe depression one moment to manic energy the next.

At the time, we simply knew that he would be happy and loving one moment, then break out into fits of rage to the extent that he was taken away several times to a sanitarium. I remember watching with horror as my father pounded the walls with his fists, paced back and forth crying, smashed his fists through windows, and became physically violent to strangers. His mental illness was beyond my mother's ability to cope, and in caring for him, she had no emotional energy or ability to nurture left over to give to me or my sister.

The first family memory related to my own birth seems symbolic of what my childhood would become. My mother walked into our small home, carrying me in her arms, a newborn fresh from the hospital. My father was at home, taking care of three-year-old Sandy. My mother's first step through the door landed her in a pile of poop. Since we had no cat or dog, my mother immediately realized Sandy must have been the guilty party.

"Sandy, where are you?" Mother yelled. "Why did you do this? Get over here and clean it up now."

With me in her arms, she raced through the house. "Edgar, Edgar. Where are you? I can't leave you alone with Sandy a minute." Flinging the back door open, she spotted my father pulling weeds from our vegetable patch. "How come you weren't watching her?"

Daddy hurried in from the backyard, scowling as he wiped a shirt sleeve over his sweaty brow. "I've been raking leaves and pulling weeds. Someone has to tend our garden. What happened?"

"You should have been in the house watching Sandy. She's a terrible girl, always up to mischief."

When I was old enough to understand, Sandy would recount this scene to me in graphic detail, smirking as she insisted she'd done it deliberately to make clear her feelings about a new baby sister. Her taunting increased once I'd graduated from a crib to share the same bed with her. She took delight in scaring me by dressing up as a ghost with a sheet over her head, holding an ominous-looking pronged garden fork in one hand. Or she would make frightening scratching noises on the wall.

"Is that you, Sandy?" I would call out, only to be answered with stony silence. Of course, the sun rose and set on schedule, and I grew in size and age. Due to a late cut-off date at that time for starting school, I was still just four years old when the time came for me to start kindergarten, but I was eager to go to school. The first day of school arrived with an alarm clock blasting in my ears. Since Sandy's upper grade school bus wouldn't come until an hour after mine, she reset the alarm and went back to sleep as I rubbed my eyes into wakefulness and jumped out of bed.

Mother came dashing in the bedroom. "I'm glad to see you're up. Put on Sandy's blue dress that she's outgrown. I'll have oatmeal waiting for you."

"I don't like that dress," I responded.

"You have no choice," she said with her hands on her hips.

My legs kicked nervously under the kitchen table as I gulped down oatmeal. Mother was taking bread out of the cupboard. "I'm making you a peanut butter and jelly sandwich for your lunch."

As she put the sandwich in a plastic baggie, I asked, "Why do I need to take the bus by myself? Can't you come with me?"

She handed me the sandwich. "There's no reason to be afraid. As soon as you get off the bus, someone will be there to take you to your classroom."

"I wish Daddy was here. He's been gone for two days."

"Don't worry, he'll be home soon," Mother answered.

My eyes watered. "But it's my first day of school. I want Daddy here. He didn't even say goodbye!"

Inhaling a sharp breath, Mother looked away without answering. When the kitchen clock showed 7:30 a.m., Mother and I walked to the bus stop in silence. A few other children and parents were waiting for the bus as well, including my friend Jenny. A large yellow school bus turned the corner and stopped in front of us. With a flurry of hug and kisses from their parents, the other children boarded the bus.

I looked over at my mother. Her arms were stiff by her side. "I'll be at the bus stop when you get off." She turned and walked away.

My head hung low as I followed Jenny downheartedly up the bus steps. *Why doesn't Mother ever give me hugs or kisses? She never says she loves me like the other mothers either.*

I scooted into a window seat next to Jenny. As the bus began to move, I spotted another little girl running towards the bus. I started yelling, "It's my friend Lynette. Stop the bus!"

The driver stopped. Lynette jumped on the bus, breathing fast and hard. She squeezed in next to Jenny and me. "I thought I'd miss the bus. Our dog ran out of the house, trying to follow me to school."

Jenny jumped up and down in her seat. "My dog did the same thing. Do you have a dog, Sue?"

I looked down at my hands. "We had a cat once, but my mother got rid of it. She said she was allergic to cats." The cat had lived outside, and my mother had never bothered to go near it, so I couldn't understand why it had to go. But when my mother made up her mind, no one dared argue, not even my father.

Lynette wrinkled her nose. "Your mother sounds mean."

I didn't know how to answer, so made no response. After several more stops, the bus pulled up to a sprawling red brick school house.

Jenny touched the window with her finger. "Hey, look at that giant sandbox. And those swings."

There were monkey bars, slides, and a tether ball as well. Lynette was already out of her seat. "I can't wait to play."

We followed her out of the bus. As we ran towards the playground, a young woman walked briskly towards us, a sheet of paper in her hand. She was tall and thin with long, flowing blonde hair and blue eyes. With a wide smile, she said, "Welcome to Lemon Grove School. My name is Mrs. Morgan, but the kids call me Mrs. Sunshine. I'm here to help you to your class. As I call out your name, I want you to form a straight line and follow me."

Looking down at her sheet of paper, she called out names. As I followed the other children in line toward our classroom, I ran my fingers through my snarled hair, feeling suddenly self-conscious of my hair and Sandy's second-hand dress that was too long. Jenny had already entered the classroom, which had white plaster walls and a hardwood floor. Several large windows looked out onto the school's grassy lawn.

"Come on, Sue." Jenny waved at me as she slid into a desk in the back corner. "You can sit next to me."

I gave her a grateful smile, but my feet felt anchored to the floor. Then a slightly plump woman with dark hair in a bun and glasses came over to me. "I'm Mrs. Jones, your new teacher." She reached out a warm hand to grasp mine. "Come on in. Your friend saved a seat for you. You can sit next to her, but no talking is allowed. Do you think you can do that?"

"Yes, Mrs. Jones." Once I scooted into my desk, I felt more comfortable. I looked over at Jenny. "Isn't this great? We have our own desks."

The teacher looked over at me and put her fingers to her lips. *Uh, oh, I'd better be quiet!* Straightening up, I folded my hands in front of me and looked around at large posters of the alphabet, numbers, planets, and animals that covered our walls. *Daddy already taught me the alphabet and how to count to ten.*

Turning my head, I saw building blocks, puzzles, finger paints, and games stacked on shelves against the wall. More than I'd ever seen in my life. *This is going to be fun. I think I'll like school.*

Mrs. Jones passed out mimeographed papers with numbered dots to connect to form a picture. I swung my legs back and forth as I connected the dots. Looking over at Jenny, I whispered, "Look, it turned into a bear."

After we finished the picture, we were given another paper where we were to match animal parts. I recognized all the animals. I was matching the lion's head to its body when the recess bell rang. Forgetting my unfinished paper, I hurried to line up behind Jenny at the door. "Let's see if we can get to the swings first."

"Can I play with you too?" Lynette called, racing behind us toward the playground.

"Sure," I said. "Let's see who can swing high enough to touch the sky."

After unsuccessful attempts and tired legs, we headed for the hopscotch squares, pretending to be grasshoppers as we leaped from one square to another. I was having so much fun that I was disappointed when the final bell signaled school was over. But I recovered quickly once Lynette, Jenny, and I boarded the bus. Sitting between Lynette and Jenny, I felt popular, liked.

When we arrived at our own bus stop, I spotted Mother waiting with the other parents. She was talking, laughing, throwing her head back in fun. *Mother is never like that with me! She always looks so sad and tired. I guess she is happy sometimes, but just not around me. How can I make her smile like that?*

Once the bus stopped, my friends ran into the open arms of waiting mothers who showered them with hugs and kisses. I could hear them asking, "How was your first day at school? What did you do? Do you like your new teacher?"

I looked over at mother. She looked unapproachable, arms tightly folded. "I hope you had a good day," she said, but her expression didn't look as though she meant it.

Mother walked with Jenny and Lynette's mothers ahead of us three kindergartners. Their heads turned back and forth in animated conversation, their arms swinging. Behind them, Jenny, Lynnette, and I entertained ourselves jumping over cracks and kicking rocks. But once we left the others, my mother and I walked the rest of the way home in an uncomfortable silence.

Our house was always neat and clean with pictures hung on white walls and rag rugs scattered on wooden floors. But it smelled stuffy and stale as we entered. This was because

Mother always kept the windows shut to avoid the outside air, which she believed would aggravate her allergies.

As we walked into the kitchen, I handed Mother my first school papers. "Look at what I did in school today!"

Mother picked the papers up, looked at them briefly, and put them down. "I didn't know you knew your numbers and could color in the lines. Good job."

With no expression, she walked away. My shoulders slumped. Hurrying down the hall into the bedroom I shared with Sandy, I yanked my dress over my head, dropped it on the floor, put on my jeans and a T-shirt, and headed for the back yard. All the excitement and fun of my first day of school had drained away.

Where is my daddy? Daddy loves me! I bet he'd play a game with me and be happy to see me! Why isn't he home?

I would learn soon enough that my father's return home was not the solution I fantasized to all the problems of my small world.

CHAPTER THREE

RESILIENCE

But now, O Lord you are our Father: we are the clay.
And you are our potter; we are all the work of your
hand.

—Isaiah 64:8

Even at the age of four, my escape from trouble and
hurt was the wide, beautiful world of nature I
could see right outside my own back door. If I
knew nothing then about God, still I could see
God's handiwork smiling down on me, dependable and
consistent. Blue skies, marshmallow clouds, delicate flowers,
bird's songs, and any creepy-crawly thing to discover and
follow brought me childish delight and made my downcast
spirit soar.

I forgot my mother's cool reception as I bent down low to
watch the ants that could be seen everywhere. Marching in
a straight line, they carried dead insects and other large
bundles to their tunneled home on a mound in the grass. My
father had told me they could carry up to five thousand times

their weight. Wandering around the yard, I spotted spider webs. *Daddy says their webs are made from silk and are stronger than steel. That's how they capture food. Oh, where is he? Why doesn't he come home?*

"Sue!" Mother's voice sliced through the air, startling me. "It's dinner time. Come home."

The mention of food sent me galloping home. The scent of pot roast greeted me at the door. Mother was in the kitchen, stirring butter into a dish of green beans.

"When's Daddy coming home?" I demanded.

"He'll be here for dinner."

Overjoyed, I ran outside to wait for Daddy's 1944 Chevrolet car to drive down the street. My mother yelled after me, "Come back here and help set the table."

Reluctantly, I obeyed. I was setting a Pyrex dish of beans on our round glass kitchen table while Sandy brought in a basket of rolls when Daddy opened the back door. Sandy and I rushed to greet him with hugs and kisses. Mother looked on with a smile. We scooted our chairs in around the table, Daddy to my right, Sandy to my left, and Mother across from me. Daddy nudged me with an elbow and patted Sandy on the back, his green eyes dancing with merriment.

"I'm so glad you're home. I missed you." As I spoke, my hands flew up in excitement, knocking over my milk.

My mother jumped to her feet furiously. "You are so clumsy," she yelled at me. "Clean it up."

My head hung low. After all my anticipation, I'd ruined my father's return. But Daddy just smiled. "That's okay."

Together he and I mopped up the milk with our napkins. My spirits lifting, I loaded my potatoes with margarine. As I ate, Daddy nudged me again. "So how was your first day of school?"

Finally, someone was interested! "It was fun. I did numbers, colored, and played games with my friends Jenny and Lynnette."

"Did you bring home any papers?"

"Oh, yes!" In my animated response, I spilled my milk again. I began to sob.

"Hey, it was just an accident." Daddy immediately comforted me. My father had a way of settling things, making things better.

After dinner, I helped clear the table, scraping any left-over food from the dishes. As I placed them on the kitchen counter to be washed, Daddy picked up a dishtowel and playfully snapped it behind me. Shrieking in delight, I grabbed the towel and jumped into his arms. "Daddy, teach me how to do that, please, please."

Sandy pulled the towel away from me. "Me too!"

We watched Daddy fold one corner of the towel in a triangle. Rolling it into a tight tube, he snapped it like a whip. Sandy copied Daddy, making a cracking sound, and squealed in delight. But though I tried many times to snap the towel, it didn't make a noise.

"Daddy, I can't do anything!" I sobbed.

"Don't give up," he chuckled, patting me on the back. "Practice makes perfect."

While Daddy, Mother, and Sandy did dishes and cleaned the floor, I headed for my bedroom to play with my paper dolls. My favorite was beautiful, red-haired Rita Hayworth, one of the top movie stars of the day. I punched out a paper evening dress with a black taffeta evening coat from my paper-doll book. Deciding she was tired, I then changed Rita into floral lounging pajamas with a hot-pink sash.

"It's seven o'clock," Mother announced from the living-room. "S*ergeant Preston of the Yukon* is about to begin."

Putting away my paper doll and her clothes, I raced into the living-room and jumped onto the couch next to Daddy. He laughed as I bounced up and down. Mother and Sandy sat next to us in straight-back chairs, looking as stiff as the chairs. *I don't think Mother likes Sandy either. They never seem to laugh or have any fun together.*

Sitting quietly, we gave rapt attention to our Lowboy console radio. Footsteps echoed in our ears as we followed the action of the mounted police, Sergeant Preston, and his sled dog, King, who helped injured trappers and captured smugglers. I liked the show even more than *Dick Tracy, Li'l Abner,* or *Little Orphan Annie.* I looked over at Daddy. That was when I noticed the glazed look in his wide-opened eyes. He was staring across the room at the far wall.

"Are you okay?" I asked.

He didn't answer, but Mother immediately spoke up. "Time for bed, girls."

"We're not tired," Sandy protested.

"It's past your bedtime. You need to go to bed."

Unhappily, Sandy and I headed to our bedroom.

"Let's wear our Christmas pajamas," I suggested.

"Let's see who can put them on first," Sandy answered.

My sister won. I leapt into bed with a high jump to miss any monsters hiding under the bed. Sandy leaned over to ask, "Are you tired?"

"No." I felt wide awake, but I was still worried. "Do you think Daddy's okay?"

"Why?"

"He looked funny."

"Oh, he's fine. There's a flashlight in the drawer. Let's turn it on under the covers and tell stories." Shining the flashlight on her face, Sandy inched closer to me. "I'm going to teach you a story I learned from Daddy. He learned it from his daddy when he was just a little boy."

I giggled, clapping my hands with excitement, as she began, "Once upon a time, a goose drank wine. A monkey chewed tobacco on a street-car line. The street-car broke, the monkey choked, and they all went to heaven on a little tin boat."

We drifted off to sleep with a smile on our faces, but I woke up screaming. Sandy shook me to quiet me down. "What's wrong?"

"Daddy turned into a monster," I wailed.

"What do you mean?"

"His face looked angry. He yelled and cried and beat his fists on the walls. I wanted to yell, but I couldn't."

Sandy shook her head. "It was only a dream. Don't think about it. You know Daddy would never do that."

But of course that wasn't true, and I knew it.

CHAPTER FOUR

TENACITY

He calmed the raging storm, and the waves became quiet.

—Psalm 107:29

That wasn't the last nightmare brought on by my father's odd behavior and strange glazed look. But as the weeks passed, he seemed better, and my nightmares gradually disappeared. At this point, Sandy and I still didn't know what was wrong with Daddy or why he'd occasionally gone away. But he'd now been home without incident for several months, and I was now in the second semester of kindergarten.

My spirits remained happy until one evening when Daddy didn't come home for dinner. As Mother served up our food in stony silence, Sandy asked, "Where's Daddy?"

"He's sick. He had to leave," Mother said. "I need to leave too. I will be visiting my mother in Santa Rosa. I've made arrangements for you to stay with some friends of mine. They'll take you to school."

Santa Rosa, my mother's home town, was north of San Francisco, a good eight to ten hours' drive from San Diego. My mother came from a large Italian clan, second and third generation immigrants by that time. My maternal grandfather had a respectable job as manager of a warehouse, but none of my mother's relatives were educated, and my grandmother was barely literate in English.

My mother's high intelligence and the scholarships she'd earned had allowed her to escape into a very different world. Whatever her outward relationship with her family, she made clear to Sandy and me that she considered herself a cut above her blue-collar relatives. In fact, she displayed nothing but contempt for her Italian heritage, which she dismissed as low-class and uneducated. At most, we would travel as a family to visit them once a year, and they in turn only came to visit us a few times. Sandy and I never really got to know any of them well. But we did have two girl cousins, daughters of our Aunt Teresa, with whom we enjoyed playing on those rare visits. So we couldn't see why Mother should leave us behind. Unless she just didn't want us around!

"You can't leave us!" Sandy cried out, grabbing my mother around the waist. I just ran into the bedroom and shut the door. Grabbing my blue stuffed teddy bear off the closet floor, I flung myself on the bed and cried.

But the week that Mother was gone didn't turn out so badly. Her friends, Mr. and Mrs. Fletcher, took good care of us and filled our days with praises for our good behavior. Mother came home without a smile. *Her friends liked me! How come she doesn't?* I asked myself.

Of course, I had no idea my mother was dealing with my father's bipolar disorder. But I did tell my mother about my nightmares and how Daddy had turned into something scary. Looking stricken, she put her hand over her mouth. "Don't think about them."

Without another word, she turned her back to me. I felt abandoned, all alone in my fears. Sandy wasn't any help. By now she was learning to keep to herself, wrapped in her own cocoon of protection. Daddy was gone for three weeks. When he finally came home, I leaped into his arms. But things weren't the same anymore. The feeling of joy, happiness, and safety at being in my father's arms was no longer there.

Daddy looked at me with questioning eyes. "Is everything okay?"

Instead of answering, I gave an exasperated shrug. I couldn't explain why I felt the way I did. But at least going to school still brought me relief. Jenny, Lynette, and I walked toward the bus stop swinging hands, skipping over cracks in the sidewalk, and playing tag.

Once we reached the school, I strolled into my classroom, shoved my lunch pail in its designated cubby hole, lifted the top of my desk, and looked over my books and papers. Then, trying to be noticed as a good student, I sat erect with my hands folded on my desk. When Mrs. Jones looked at me and smiled, I smiled widely back.

But even school didn't remain a refuge. Shortly after my father's return, I threw up during nap time. I wiped it up quickly with my dress, hoping no one would notice. But another girl yelled, "What's that smell? It stinks!"

She pointed her finger at me. "I think Sue threw up on the carpet!"

The school nurse took my temperature, then had me lay down on a hard, narrow bed in the nurse's office while she called my mother to come pick me up and take me home. By the time she arrived, I'd thrown up again. Sliding into the car, I slumped over, holding my stomach. Mother's face was pinched into a scowl. "I hope you're not getting polio."

"Why, Mother?"

"It's a terrible disease."

My aching insides churned all the way home. With an expression of disdain, Mother fed me a tablespoon of cod liver oil, then gave me a mustard pack for my stomach pain. She drew the curtains as I fell into bed. Gloom filled the air.

The next day I woke up with a fresh spurt of energy. Bright sun slanting through the curtains wove geometric shapes on the wall. I ran into the kitchen, ready for some cereal. Mother was standing over the sink, washing dishes. She turned around, blew her nose, and wiped her eyes.

"What's wrong?" I asked in alarm.

"Daddy had to leave again."

"Why?"

"He's still sick. He came home too soon."

"Is he going to die?"

"No. His sickness is in his mind." Her head bowed, Mother blew her nose again, turned her back to me, and continued doing the dishes. My chest ached. *What's wrong with my Daddy? How come he didn't say good-by? Did I do something wrong?*

"My stomach doesn't hurt any more. Can I go outside?" Grabbing a couple of cookies, I charged out the back door, breathing deeply of Nature's life-giving force. The following day, I felt well enough to go back to school, swinging my hands along with Jenny and Lynette as we made our way to the bus.

"What does your mother have for you when you come home from school?" Jenny asked Lynette. "My mother usually has home baked cookies."

"Mine asks about my day, school work, things I did," Lynette answered.

I remained silent, tightening the barrette in my hair. *I'm not important enough to expect any attention. Maybe it would be different if I work really hard and bring home some papers with gold stars. That might make Mother happy. I know Daddy would be proud of me. When is he coming home?*

That day after school, I ran into the house, calling out, "Mother, I got some gold stars today."

Dead silence. My feet went flying down the hall. Stopping by my parents' closed bedroom door, I tapped hesitantly.

"What do you want?" she called out harshly.

"Will you look at my school papers? I got a hundred percent on my spelling test, and I drew a picture of a red bird. The teacher even put a gold star on the top of my paper. Will you look at them?"

"Put the papers on the kitchen table. I'll look at them in a minute."

Wandering into the kitchen, I tossed my papers on the table. *Maybe my papers aren't worth looking at.* Heading into my bedroom, I changed out of my school clothes and flew out the back door. The outdoors met me with open arms. Here at least I could escape into my childhood adventures and wild imagination.

I became a bird, flapping my arms. I climbed up trees like a monkey. I chased grasshoppers, as they hopped away. Finding a lady bug dressed with its colorful red spots, I picked it up gently, chanting, "Ladybug, ladybug, fly away home. Your house is on fire, and your children are doomed." I moved my hand slightly as its little black wings took flight, carrying my good wishes with it.

There was always something fun to do in my outdoor playground. Some days I caught white, yellow, and golden butterflies with my net. I always let them go unharmed, not touching their wings for fear of damaging them. Sometimes I made pets out of insects, capturing them in mason jars. I would add dirt and a few leaves, then watch in fascination as they crawled around their new home. I made lids out of wax paper and cut holes so the insects could get air.

I was often interrupted by a train whistle. Stopping whatever I was doing, I would race through the open field behind our house, stopping by a quarry that edged against low hills to listen to the vibration of the railroad ties. When the train finally came around the bend, I would jump up and down, waving frantically until the conductor in his striped cap noticed me and waved back.

On this day as the sun slipped into the west, I rushed home, hoping that despite what Mother had told me, Daddy would be there. Flying through the back screen door, I called, "Daddy, are you home?"

Mother was sitting in the kitchen, her head bowed, darning socks. She looked up, her mouth set in a hard line. "Your father still isn't here."

"When's he coming home?"

"I don't know."

The next day was Saturday. Still no Daddy. Mother disappeared behind the closed door of their bedroom. Sandy showed up only at meals. I escaped outside to meet up with Lynette and Jenny in the large open field that adjoined our backyards. We chased each other, pretending to be wild, crazy animals. Once our energy was spent, we went to Jenny's house. I loved going there. Her mother smiled, sometimes even gave me a hug. And, unlike my house, her curtains were open. The sun cast happy beams throughout the house.

The three of us went into Jenny's bedroom. Sprawling on the floor, we played with paper dolls, completed puzzles, and built tall buildings with blocks. I knew Jenny and Lynnette liked me. I liked them too. But they rarely came over to my house. I hated it when they asked, "Why can't we go over to your house?"

"My house isn't any fun," I would respond. *Why would anyone want to come to my house? It's a sad place. Dark. No fun. And I don't have any games to play.*

I was no longer interested in the game of *Chutes and Ladders* we were playing. "I want to go home. Maybe Daddy's there."

"Doesn't your father live with you?" Jenny asked.

"Yes, but he's gone a lot."

"Why?" Lynette asked.

I gave a half shrug.

But the days continued to pass with no Daddy coming home at 6:00 p.m. from his law office. I missed jumping into the car with him as he drove up the driveway, walking backwards on his feet down the hall when he was in a good mood. One day after school, I was staring out of my bedroom window when I spotted a white, brown, and orange calico cat in our backyard. When I hurried outside, the cat ran over to me, rubbing herself against my legs and purring. I dashed into the house and brought out some milk. The cat must have been hungry as she lapped the milk right up.

I named the cat Patches and secretly fed her milk and scraps of food. I didn't dare tell mother. She might take the cat away. Sandy said she'd keep my secret and had fun playing with her too. Patches became my companion and best friend until Mother noticed me carrying out some milk on a platter.

"What are you doing?" she yelled.

"Nothing."

Following me out, she saw the cat run towards me. "You can't keep that cat."

"Why?" My eyes welled up in tears.

"I'm allergic," she said through a slit for a mouth.

I knotted my fists. "You took away my last cat. I'm five years old now. I'll take good care of her."

She turned away, ignoring my pleas. I went to bed that night with the covers over my head, trying to stifle uncontrollable whimpering. I woke up early and ran outside, frantically searching for my cat. Giving up, I finally went back inside, where I threw myself on my bed and dissolved into tears.

I was outside, seeking comfort from Nature, when I heard Daddy's car coming up the driveway. Meeting him in the garage, I jumped into his arms and told him about mother taking away my cat.

His eyes narrowed. "You know your mother."

At the dinner table that night, Daddy was very quiet. The whites of his eyes seemed overly enlarged as he stared blankly across the room.

"Daddy, Daddy," I said. "Are you okay?"

He didn't answer. The rest of my dinner tasted like cardboard. The next day I thought I would surprise him when he came home from work. Climbing to the top of a fig tree that would be in Daddy's view when he drove up, I made cat-like noises I thought would bring a smile to his face. But he didn't arrive at his usual time. After waiting what seemed like an hour, I climbed down the tree and ran into the house, looking for mother. She was in the garage, bent over washing clothes.

"How come Daddy didn't come home from work?" I demanded.

"He's still sick," Mother said.

My eyes watered. "What does that mean? Is he in a hospital? Is he going to die?"

Mother pummeled the dirty clothes. "No, he's not that kind of sick. He's in a sanitarium."

"What's that?"

"It's for people who are sad. When he's happy, he will be home again."

"How come he didn't say goodbye?"

"I don't know."

I thought I knew why! *Daddy doesn't like me,* I told myself bitterly. Over the next weeks I slipped into a despairing fog. I missed Daddy's twinkling, loving eyes. I missed him sitting next to me at the dinner table, talking about everyday stuff. Without him, Mother, Sandy, and I just sat around the table like strangers with no words exchanged. I missed his snapping towel and listening to radio programs sitting close to Daddy on the couch.

School was no longer a refuge to me. I stopped paying attention to the point where the teacher walked over to me, hands on her hips. "Sue, can't you hear me? You need to listen to my instructions."

Every day, the school bus dropped me off into a group of parents who picked up their kids from the bus stop, showering them with love. All but me. At night, I was once again plagued with nightmares of my father throwing things, banging walls, crying in fits of despair. I would wake up drenched in sweat with a knotted stomach.

Though I would not understand for many decades what was happening to me, it was at this point that I learned to shove down my feelings, disassociating myself from the pain and trauma. Rather than dwell on a father who wasn't home and a mother who showed no concern for me, I clung fiercely to my memories of the daddy I loved. The daddy who loved me in return.

CHAPTER FIVE

SURVIVAL

> He heals the brokenhearted and binds their wounds.
>
> —Psalm 147:3

A full month after my father had left again, Mother met the bus one day after school with a wide grin and an eager wave. My heart soaring, I hurried towards her. Her folded arms warded off a hug, but at least her tone was cheerful. "Your father is coming home today."

"When?"

"He'll be home sometime before dinner."

In my exuberance, I chatted all the way home. Mother made no eye contact, so I wasn't sure if she was listening. But I continued nonstop anyway. Once at home, I hurried out to the backyard, where I perched on a rock to wait for my father, pretending I was a bird flying high up in the sky where I could escape from dangers below.

After what seemed forever, I heard Daddy's car turn into the driveway. I ran through the house to greet him. His green eyes twinkled in merriment as I hugged him around the waist, then stood on his feet so we could walk into the house as one.

This time Daddy stayed home for several months without a "sick leave". My fabric of life began mending its rips. My listening skills came back. My nightmares stopped. My playful spirit sparked alive. And my school work blossomed. Daddy was proud of me.

Then one evening we were sitting around the dinner table, passing bowls of corn, ham, and salad. Sandy passed the food to the right of her, not taking any for herself.

"What's wrong with you?" Mother asked. "You have to eat."

"I'm not feeling well." Sandy dropped her head into her hands. Pushing his chair away from the table, Daddy stood up. "I'm going to check if you have a fever."

He placed his hand on Sandy's forehead. "You feel fine. No temperature." Picking up the bowl of mashed potatoes, he waggled it back and forth in front of Sandy. "Try to eat. It might help you feel better."

Sandy turned her head away. "I can't."

We finished our meal in meal in silence. As we began clearing the plates, Sandy moaned, "Mother, can I go to bed?"

"Are you trying to get out of doing the dishes?" Daddy said jokingly.

Sandy shook her head. "I really feel sick. I'm not kidding."

"Okay, you're excused," Mother said.

I stayed in the kitchen to help Daddy clear the table, then charged up to the bedroom Sandy and I shared to check on my sister. She was sitting up in bed, reading a Superman comic book. I sighed in relief. "Looks like you're feeling better."

"I am. Let's make a tent in the bed and tell stories."

The white sheets smelled like soap as we pulled them over our heads, letting our imaginations took flight. We slid up and down red, orange, yellow, and green stripped rainbows, looking for pots of gold. We stood up on the backs of white horses in a circus and climbed beanstalks like *Jack in the Beanstalk*.

"Do you really think there's a pot of gold at the end of rainbows?" I asked Sandy.

"No, but no one knows for sure."

"Do you think we could find a magic seed, plant it, and have it grow really tall?"

"No, but we can pretend."

The next morning, I woke up to a blood-curdling scream. Sandy was on the floor, trying to stand up.

"Sandy, what's wrong?" I yelled. "Look at your feet. They're all twisted."

"I don't know," she cried.

I rushed out of the room. "Mother, Mother, come look at Sandy."

Mother was soon helping my sister to the car. Sandy lay across the back seat, an alarmed, pained look on her face. I sat in the front seat, tears streaming down my face. Was my sister going to die? I didn't want to lose her.

When we reached the hospital, Mother and I helped Sandy out of the car, holding onto both her arms, and headed into the hospital lobby, barely managing to open the front door. The receptionist looked bright and cheerful in a black and cream polka-dotted blouse. "How can I help you?"

"My daughter can't walk," Mother sobbed. "Her legs are twisted. I think she has polio."

The receptionist's eyes widened in horror. Now largely extinct, thanks to the vaccine that was introduced in 1955, polio was a highly contagious disease that caused paralysis and many other conditions, leaving countless children and adults crippled for life. Grabbing a tissue, the receptionist covered her nose as though protecting herself against contagion. "Have a seat in the waiting room. You'll be called shortly."

We plopped down on a couch until a nurse arrived. Asking Mother and I to follow her, the nurse took Sandy's arm and assisted her into an examination room. After a brief wait, a doctor walked in, wearing a long, white jacket. A stethoscope hung from his neck. He checked Sandy's neck for swollen glands, her back for stiffness, her reflexes, and if she swallowed and breathed easily.

He then picked up his chart and began writing down notes as he shook his head. "I think she better spend the night. We need to do more tests, but I think she has polio."

The next day, Sandy was officially diagnosed with polio. Our whole family was scared. The neighbors were scared. The school was scared. Polio was a scourge that terrified everyone. About twenty-five percent of those afflicted suffered mild disabilities, but another twenty-five percent were left with serious disabilities, such as paralysis of the arms and legs. Death was also a possibility.

Even though Sandy remained in the hospital, a quarantine sign was posted on our front door. This meant I couldn't go to school and we couldn't receive any visitors. My father had been out of town when Sandy was diagnosed and wasn't allowed to come home. Mother kept the curtains drawn, so that the house felt like a dark tomb.

Once again, I found my own escape in the open fields behind our house. The beauty of Nature helped me feel a part of something bigger than our family's current problems. Leaves swayed in the wind. The sun found its way through the clouds. Rocks of various sizes and colors waited to be discovered. Sometimes I piled stones into a small mound, caught various small insects to place on top, and watched in fascination as they crawled up, down, and around.

But just two days after Sandy had been admitted to the hospital, I came indoors to hear my mother talking on the phone. "What? She's not even allowed to go outside? I had no idea it was that contagious." There was a pause. "Okay, I'll see that she stays in."

I wanted to run the other way, but my mother had already spotted me. For the next three weeks, she kept me in the house, watching me, following me. With no way to escape, my mind reverted to a blank slate, not seeing, feeling or caring. Again, I was learning to cope by disassociating myself from my emotions and surroundings.

CHAPTER SIX

PEACE

My presence will go with you, and I will give you rest.
—Exodus 33:13

W e finally received a call that Sandy was better and could come home. Our quarantine sign was taken down. Mother and I jumped into the car and sped to the hospital. I raced ahead of Mother into Sandy's room. My sister was sitting up in bed. "Finally, I can have some company."

Rushing over, I gave Sandy a hug, then parked myself on the corner of her bed. "It's been so terrible without you. And Daddy's been gone too."

"Why?" Sandy asked.

Mother had now entered the room. "He was at work when you got sick and wasn't allowed to come home."

I grabbed a pillow off Sandy's bed and hugged it. "What's it like in the hospital?"

"Terrible," Sandy said. "They made me eat hard-boiled eggs. I hate them. They carried me to the bathroom like a baby. Sometimes I couldn't stand it anymore and tried to get out of bed by myself. My legs were so weak, I fell each time."

Mother began gathering up Sandy's belongings. A nurse in a white dress, apron, and cap came in pushing a wheelchair. Helping Sandy into the wheelchair, she pushed her down the halls and out the front door of the hospital, where she lifted Sandy into the front seat of my mother's car.

"You're still a little weak," she admonished Sandy. "You'll have to take it easy for a while. Your mother has a list of instructions. Follow them, and you'll soon feel as good as new."

I climbed into the back seat, and we drove away in silence, my mother looking stiff and unapproachable as usual. As soon as we pulled into our garage, Sandy jumped out of the car. She almost fell, leaning against the car to regain her balance.

"I'm okay," she whimpered. "Can I go to school tomorrow?"

Mother shook her head. "The doctor said you need to regain your strength. You can't even stand up straight. Maybe in a week."

I jumped up and down. "I can go to school, can't I?"

"Yes. You'll be given three weeks of catch-up work. And you can bring Sandy's home with you too."

Sandy smiled at me. "I'll help you catch up."

We linked arms and walked into the house. Mother brought out the waffle iron, and in a few minutes, we were enjoying waffles soaked in syrup and butter. When Sandy finished, she pushed her plate away. "I'm tired. I want to take a nap."

I followed her into the bedroom. "I've missed you."

"I missed you too." She smiled faintly. "So much I even felt bad scaring you all those times dressed like a ghost and grabbing your feet, pretending to be a monster. I won't do that anymore."

My sister was clearly not as recovered as she'd insisted as she immediately fell asleep. Just before dinner, I heard Daddy's car. I ran outside and jumped into his arms. *Sandy's home, and now Daddy's home!* I went to bed that night with a smile on my face. Breakfast the next morning was the best ever. Even Mother joined in the animated conversation and cast a smile my way. Daddy let me eat a few bites of pancakes and bacon off his plate. His food always tasted better than mine.

After breakfast, I rushed into the bedroom to get dressed, then flew out the door, anxious to go to school. Jenny and Lynette were waiting for me. Holding hands, we raced to the bus stop. Once I arrived at school, friends gathered around me, asking me where I'd been. It felt good to be missed. Even my teacher greeted me with a hug. I scooted into my desk and opened the top. My papers and books were still there. Everything felt good, back to its proper order.

At recess, my teacher walked towards me with a package in her hands. "Sue, I have a present for you. We missed you the last three weeks."

Opening the package, I found three soaps: yellow, pink, and white. They smelled like a bouquet of flowers. I was thrilled.

By now my first school year was almost over. Those final weeks were good ones. With my sister and father both home, our family was once again complete. Daddy helped me with my homework and my reading. He also taught me to ride a bicycle. We even went to a nearby church a few times.

We'd never been to church before as a family, and my parents never told Sandy and me why we were suddenly spending Sunday mornings this way. But I could see that Daddy loved standing out in front after the service, pumping people's hands and exchanging good-natured introductions. My mother would stand by, smiling sweetly, but never saying a word. Seeing her smile brought a heaviness to my chest, as at home I only saw her frown.

When Daddy and Mother headed into the church service, Sandy and I would follow our Sunday school teacher to a classroom. There we learned about a God who had created the world and who loved and protected us. I clung to those teachings, yearning for such comfort in the dark of the night when nightmares came to life and monsters threatened.

But my new-found sense of peace and order came crashing down when Daddy announced one Sunday morning over a breakfast of pancakes loaded with syrup and butter, "We'll be moving in a few weeks. You'll love the house. It's much bigger than this."

"But I like this house," I wailed. "And what about my friends?"

"Mine too!" Sandy chimed in. "And what about school? Will we have to change schools?"

"Yes," Daddy answered. "Your new school is so close to our new home that you'll be able to walk. It'll be much better than taking a bus."

"You're going to be fine," Mother interjected. "You can make new friends."

"We'll drive by the house tomorrow," Daddy assured Sandy and me. "You'll like it, I promise."

My mood lightened a bit. The next day we pulled up in front of our new house. La Mesa, where my father had grown up and where we'd lived as a family to this point, was in San Diego County, but some distance from the actual city of San

Diego, where he maintained his law practice. Our new house was within the actual San Diego city limits, a two-story edifice with a few scraggly bushes in the front and one small tree in the middle of a brown-spotted lawn.

A shadow crossed Sandy's face. "Yuck! I like our old house better."

Mother stiffened. "Now girls, this house is much better. It cost a lot of money, so I don't want to hear any complaints."

"Can we go inside?" I asked.

"Nobody's home to let us in," Daddy said. "But your mother and I have checked it over. You're going to love it."

My kindergarten year ended. A few weeks later, a U-Haul truck pulled up in front of our house. Running outside, Sandy and I and gawked at it with an open mouth. Mother came out of the house behind us, struggling with a heavy box. "You two. Go in your bedroom and empty your drawers. You'll find empty boxes in the hall to pack."

Running into the house, I found my favorite teddy bear and carried it outside, wiping my wet eyes on the bear. Daddy was standing by the U-Haul. "Daddy, can I keep my bear with me?"

"Sure," he said, patting me on the back.

A couple days later, Sandy and I climbed into the back seat of Daddy's car, crowded on both sides with boxes, and peered out of the windows as our house and neighborhood disappeared from sight. Sandy looked over at me. "Are you sad?"

I nodded. "I'm going to miss my friends."

Sandy looked down. "Me too."

A half-an-hour later, Daddy pulled into the garage of our new home. Piling out of the car, Sandy and I raced into the house to check it out. Inside, we discovered a large kitchen, breakfast nook, dining room, powder room, and a downstairs bedroom. Opposite the kitchen, which was by the back door, was a wash room with a large farm sink for hand-scrubbing and room for our wringer washing machine.

"Let's go upstairs," Sandy suggested. Jumping two steps at a time, we barged through two large bedrooms and an adjoining bathroom. We were thrilled to discover an outside balcony.

"Wow, look how high we are," Sandy said. "And look, there's a canyon we can explore right over there."

"Sandy, do you know which bedroom is ours?"

"Ask Mother."

I yelled, "Mother, what bedroom are we sleeping in?"

"You're sleeping downstairs," she yelled back. "Sandy has one of the bedrooms upstairs."

I looked into the bedroom that had been assigned to Sandy. The furnishings were not those we'd had in our bedroom at our old house, but brand-new, including twin beds. With two beds, it certainly seemed there would be room for me. I held back tears as I raced downstairs. I found my mother in the kitchen, putting away some dinnerware. "I'm going to be downstairs by myself?"

Mother didn't even look up. "You'll be okay."

My whole body was now prickling with fear. Nightmares had so often plagued my sleep, but at least I'd always woken up to Sandy sharing my bedroom and my fears. "Where's Daddy?"

"In the garage."

I dashed into the garage. My father was bent over, unpacking boxes. "Daddy, am I going to sleep downstairs by myself?"

Daddy looked up, his green eyes clouded with concern. "That's the way your mother wants it."

"But . . . I'm scared to be by myself. Can't I sleep in Sandy's room?"

He shrugged his shoulders. "Talk to your mother."

Stifling a cry, I darted up the steps back into the house. *If only I could crawl in a hole and die.* Running through the house, I called out, "Mother, Mother, where's my teddy bear?"

"Don't sound so panicked," she called back. "I put it on the top of a box in your bedroom."

Finding the downstairs bedroom where my boxes had been placed, I grabbed up my blue teddy bear. The furniture had already been set up in my new bedroom. It was brand-new as well. But that didn't cheer me up. Throwing myself on the bed, I rocked back and forth, arms wrapped tightly around my bear. Then Mother came barreling in. "You need to unpack your boxes."

Feeling numb, I began sorting through my belongings. That night, dinner felt lifeless, dead. The baked potatoes, lamb, and corn had no taste and went into my stomach like undesired lumps.

"Sue, didn't you hear me?" Daddy said. "I asked you to pass the potatoes around the table."

"I'm sorry, Daddy. I didn't hear you," I responded.

"Are you okay?"

I wasn't okay. I felt swallowed up by the big house, alone, defenseless. But I shrugged my shoulders. "Sure."

CHAPTER SEVEN

FEAR

Be strong, do not fear; your God will come, he will
come with vengeance, with divine retribution he will
come to save you.

— Isaiah 35:4

A dark cloud of fear followed me into my bedroom
that night. I jumped into bed and pulled the
covers over my head. Unfamiliar sounds filled
the night air—the creaking of the house, a
branch scraping against my window. *Why did Mother make
me sleep downstairs in this big house all by myself?*

I clamped my teeth together, holding back tears. I tried to
focus on what the Sunday school teacher had taught us
about a God who lived out there in the dark night and could
protect me. But as I drifted to sleep, the scraping of the
branch against my window turned into a monster with red
eyes and blood-covered skin. I lay frozen in my solitary bed,
my heart pounding against my chest. Then, unable to stand
it any longer, I threw the covers back, jumped out of bed,

thundered up the stairs, and charged into my parents' bedroom.

Hurrying to Daddy's side of the bed, I shook him into wakefulness. He rubbed his eyes and sat up. "What is it?"

"A monster is outside, scratching against my window."

He climbed out of bed and headed downstairs. "Stay here."

Ignoring his command, I tiptoed behind Daddy and watched trembling from the doorway as he opened my bedroom curtains. He turned around with a smile. "There's nothing to be scared of. It's only an oleander tree brushing against your window." "Ca-ca-can I sleep with you?"

"Just for the first night. You need to adjust to sleeping downstairs by yourself."

My eyes moistened. "I don't understand why I can't I sleep with Sandy like we did before."

His eyebrows pinched together, "Ask your mother."

I didn't. Why bother! My parents did let me sleep with them the first couple of nights. Then I had to retreat to my own bedroom, where monsters lurked under my bed, in the closet, and in each unnamed shadow. When I told Mother of my fears, she bought me a night light to quiet my imagination. It didn't help. I felt as though my fears and pain were being dismissed as not important enough to merit attention.

The day before the next school year was due to start, I woke up to hear kids shrieking, giggling, and laughing outside my house. Running into the living-room, I peeked through the curtains. Outside in the street, a number of kids were playing kickball. I wondered if any of them would be in my class. Maybe even become a new friend.

"Hey, look, there's kids playing," Sandy announced behind me. "Shall we join them?"

"No, I've been wanting to explore that canyon behind our house."

"Hey, sure, that's a good idea."

Grabbing some cookies from the kitchen, Sandy and I ran across our back yard, opened the gate, and headed down an embankment. We'd both picked up some scratches on our legs by the time we reached the bottom of the canyon. There a creek meandered through a carpet of green studded with an occasional mushroom and the full, round white clouds of ripe dandelions.

"This is beautiful," I said breathlessly.

Sandy began untying her shoes. "Let's wade a bit."

Sitting down, we took off our shoes and let our feet dangle in the cool, rushing creek water while we ate our cookies. We then walked along the stream, picking dandelions and blowing at their white fluff. We finally headed home, climbing up the embankment and back through the gate into our own backyard.

That evening as the four of us sat down to supper, I chatted animatedly between bites of food. "We saw some kids outside playing this morning. Maybe we'll see them at school. And Sandy and I found a creek down in the canyon."

Daddy smiled at me. "It sounds like you had a good day."

I glanced over at Mother. Her face was expressionless. Daddy was still talking. "Your mother and I met your new teacher, Sue. Her name is Mrs. Livingstone. She's friendly and nice. You'll like her. She's anxious to meet you."

The next morning, I hopped out of bed early and pulled on a plaid dress, eager for my first day of school. Sandy and I sat down to oatmeal and toast, then Mother handed us our lunch pails. "There's a peanut butter and jelly sandwich, an orange, and one cookie."

Daddy came down the stairs in suit and tie, ready to go to work. He gave me a hug. "Now remember, you're a first-grader now. I want to hear every detail about your first day when I get home tonight."

Daddy hurried out to catch a bus that would take him downtown to his law office. On this first day, Mother had decided to drive us to school, so Sandy and I jumped into the car, rolling down the windows so that my blond braids and Sandy's brown ponytail danced in the wind. The car stopped in front of a gray structure where swarms of kids were climbing out of cars, riding bikes, walking arm-in-arm, talking and laughing. Sandy and I sat in the car, too nervous to move.

"Come on. Out of the car." Sliding out of her seat, Mother shooed us from the car. "I'll pick you up after school, but just the first day. Otherwise you'll walk. It's only a mile away."

I grabbed my Betty Boop lunch pail while Sandy grabbed her lunch bag. Together, we walked up the school steps, through the open door, and down a long hall.

"Remember, your classroom number is 5," Sandy reminded me. "Mine is 7."

I felt lightheaded as I peered into classrooms filled with chattering strangers. "Look, Sandy. There's my classroom."

"Okay, I'll see you after school." Sandy patted my shoulder as she turned away. A woman welcomed me into my classroom with a warm smile. Showing me to my assigned seat, she introduced herself as Mrs. Livingstone. Her voice was smooth and soft like velvet.

Schoolwork always came easy to me, so I breezed through the "Dick and Jane" first-grade reading books and math assignment, earning praise from the teacher. But recess was not so easy without my friends Jenny and Lynnette at my side. Finding an isolated bench under an elm tree, I peered through some low branches to watch other children eating their sandwiches together, talking and laughing, playing on the playground equipment. I felt isolated and alone as I ate my own lunch.

But with my outgoing nature and enthusiasm for sports, it wasn't many days before I was running, shrieking, laughing, and playing with my classmates. Life was now running smoothly at school, but less so at home. I'd dash into the kitchen, opening the refrigerator for a snack as I called, "Mommy, I'm home! Do you want to look at my school papers?"

"Put them on the kitchen counter," she'd yell from upstairs in her bedroom. "I'll look at them later."

She never bothered, and her lack of interest continued to be a source of pain. But Daddy at least made me feel better with his upbeat nature. His green eyes danced as he'd spin me around in a circle or prance like a horse with me on his shoulders. He listened with interest as I read *Dick and Jane* and would read to me in turn my favorite story, *The Little Engine That Could,* who huffed and puffed, saying "I think I can, I think I can." Sprawled out on his lap as he read to me, I felt relaxed, comfortable, and loved.

My father also had a wonderful, hearty laugh that I loved. I would often lay in wait for Daddy to come home from work. Once I spotted his distinctive ambling walk heading from the car to the house, I would grab a glass of water and stand ready to splash him as he passed me. Instead of getting angry at the wetting, he would just laugh and reward me with a bear-hug.

But as my first-grade year advanced, I saw Daddy less and less. Without him, our meals were a solemn affair. Mother often scooted her chair over to the kitchen counter to eat with her back to us. When I asked where Daddy was, Mother would answer brusquely, "He's working late. His dinner will be in the oven."

Sandy's reaction to my father's increasing absence was hostility toward me. She'd kick me under the table, spill my milk, and give me the middle finger. I'd cry, "Mother, stop her. She's picking on me."

Rather than punishing Sandy, my mother would yell angrily, "You are bad girls!"

I would hang my head in shame. I needed my Daddy. Sometimes I caught a glimpse of him coming or going, looking downcast instead of the smiling, jovial person he'd been just weeks earlier. I did not understand, of course, that this was one more swing in the pendulum of his bipolar mood shifts. But my own inner darkness—a mix of fear, insecurity, and self-blame—was building into a carefully tamped-away, but engulfing vortex of emotion that sooner or later was destined to explode.

Sandy and I walked to school together, but we no longer had much fun. My sister was beginning to feel like a stranger to me. Still, once I walked into my classroom and spotted my beautifully colored pictures and "A" work the teacher often displayed on the walls, I knew that this at least was a place I belonged.

Several months into first grade, Mother announced I was going to have piano lessons. I didn't enjoy playing the piano and would have preferred to be out on the street where I could hear other kids laughing and playing while I practiced. I had to participate in music recitals. After each recital, Mother would buy me a new Storybook doll. The dolls were beautiful, dressed in long silk dresses decorated with lace and ribbons. But they were decorative rather than dolls a child would play with, and Mother always placed them up on a shelf in my bedroom that was beyond my reach, as though saying, "Look, don't touch."

My parents themselves both played the piano. I particularly enjoyed hearing Mother play *My Little Buttercup.* Uncharacteristically, she would also display a slight smile as she hummed along to the tune. But if I asked to join her on the piano bench, she would immediately rebuff me. "No, there's not enough room."

This left me feeling disconnected, not only to her, but to the music. In contrast, Daddy played the piano when he was angry. He would pound out Chopin's Polonaise up and down on the key board with fierce, rapid finger strokes.

"Daddy, are you okay?" I would ask anxiously.

But he never answered, his eyes ablaze in fury as his body rocked back and forth to the martial beats of the music. At those times, my nightmares of Daddy going crazy would flash through my mind. Retreating into my bedroom, I would slam the door shut and cover my ears with my hands, my body shaking in fear until the frightening noise stopped.

I didn't want my Daddy to go away again.

CHAPTER EIGHT

NATURE'S SOOTHING BALM

For since the creation of the world His invisible attributes, His power and nature has been clearly seen, being understood through what has been made, so that they are without excuse.

—Romans 1:20

As always, my escape was the outdoors. My own special retreat was on the northern side of the house where a shaded area about two feet wide and fifteen feet long was bordered by a Eugenia bush loaded with delicious, red berries. A soft blanket of tiny emerald-green leaves called baby tears covered the ground. Ferns gracefully drooped their lacy fronds, and Calla lilies showed off their ivory-white trumpet flowers.

This spot became my personal refuge in times of danger or trouble. But other creatures liked it too—salamanders, horny toads, other crawly things, even the occasional pet chameleon my father would bring home. I'd bend down low, pretending to be their size as I watched them climb up and over the plants or sink into the carpet of baby tears.

Sandy had her own special hide-away. One day I was outside eating an orange from one of our own fruit trees when I noticed an opened hatch along the side of our house. Walking over, I bent to look inside. The hatch led into a musty, dark, dank space underneath the house. There sat Sandy on a spread-out blue blanket, eating graham crackers.

She looked up, startled. "What are you doing here? Nobody is supposed to find me."

"Why are you in there?" I asked. "I bet it's filled with snakes and spiders."

Sandy leaned against the moist wall. "I like it here. I have it all to myself. And the kitchen is right above me. I can eavesdrop on telephone conversations and stay out of Mother's way.

"Why do you want to stay out of Mother's way?"

Sandy hung her head low. "She likes you better than me. She even calls you pet."

I sat quietly for a moment, twisting my hands. "I don't like it here. Let's go outside and play in the canyon."

"Okay, I'm tired of this. Let's go."

Sandy crawled out and shook the dirt from her clothes. Then we headed through the backyard and down the embankment. I spotted some plants with small, red balls hanging from them. They were cherry tomatoes somehow growing wild in the grass.

"Sandy, can we eat those?"

"Sure, let's grab a handful." I gathered two, while she gathered four. She offered me one. "Here, take one of mine to make it even."

This was the Sandy I remembered before her recent hostility. *Maybe she really does like me!*

"Look. There's some sour grass." Sandy pointed out a patch of the edible weed across the creek. My mouth was puckering with its tartness when I noticed what looked like a leaf lettuce plant.

"Hey, can we eat that too?"

"Sure. It's called Indian lettuce because it grows wild, and the Indians picked it for salad."

"You know everything. How come I'm so stupid?" *Maybe that's why Mother lets her wear her Phi Betta Kappa key from college, because she's so smart. Mother tells me I'm not smart enough to wear it.*

Sandy shook her head and shrugged her shoulders. "I'm three years older than you. Of course, I know more. Come on, Sue, we'd better head for home. It's getting late."

That evening Daddy came home in time for dinner. But as I looked up into his face, fear gripped me. His eyes were looking blank and wide open again with too much white showing. Twisting his cigarette in an ashtray to put it out, Daddy stared across at the far wall. Mother was passing rice, beans, and meat around the table. Daddy usually took several heaping tablespoons of each, but this time he took one small spoonful of each, then handed me the dish without so much as a glance my way.

"Daddy, are you all right?" On his other side, Sandy tapped my father on the shoulder. He made no response.

That night, I awoke to a sharp crack of thunder. Lightening lit up my room. The rain sounded like nails pounding down on my roof. I pulled the covers over my head, tossing and turning back into a fretful sleep. I could hear Mother yelling. Was I dreaming?

Then my eyes popped open. Mother stood over me, hands on her hips. "We need to take your father to the hospital."

A heartrending wailing reached me from the kitchen. Following the sound, I stopped dead in my tracks at the sight of my father pacing back and forth. He screamed out swear words, his face twisted and tormented. Fists clenched, he flailed at the air as though attacking an imaginary enemy.

Her hands shaking, Mother rummaged frantically through a stack of miscellaneous papers on her kitchen desk. Uncovering the phone-book, she thumbed rapidly through the yellow pages. The noise had now drawn Sandy downstairs as well. We both stood there, frozen in horror. I wanted to help, but didn't know how.

Mother was now speaking into the phone. "Is this the Norwalk asylum? Yes, he's very ill. He needs immediate help. Yes, we'll be there as soon as possible, hopefully in a couple of hours."

She banged the receiver down, only to pick it up again. The next number she dialed was to Daddy's friend and law partner, Mr. Goodman, who lived nearby. "Edgar is having a breakdown. Could you come over and try to calm him down?"

Sandy brushed past me, running upstairs. Dashing into my own bedroom, I threw myself down on the bed, put my fingers in my ears, and began rocking back and forth. In just a few minutes, I heard a loud pounding at the door, then footsteps entering the house.

"Thank goodness you're here!" Mother called out. "Edgar isn't responding to anything I'm saying. I hope you can help me calm him down, as I need to drive him to Norwalk Sanitarium in L.A."

Daddy's yelling dwindled into soft, indistinct sounds. Then the door slammed shut. Daddy's partner must have left.

Pushing myself up from the bed, I opened the door and tiptoed back into the kitchen. Daddy was slumped over in a kitchen chair. Mother was standing above him, hands clenched at her side. As she turned to look at me, I could see fear and distress in her eyes.

"Hurry up. Get dressed. We're taking Daddy to the sanitarium. Where's Sandy?"

"She went upstairs."

Mother hurried upstairs into Sandy's bedroom. I followed her. My sister was lying face down in her bed, crying. My mother shook her brusquely. "We have no time for that. We need to take your father to the sanitarium right away. He's having a mental breakdown."

Running back downstairs to my own bedroom, I yanked my blue flannel nightgown over my head so quickly a few buttons popped off. Not bothering to pick them up, I pulled on pants and a T-shirt. My mother was already calling, "Let's go. I'll be in the car."

As I slid into the back seat of the car, Daddy was in front of me, sitting stiff as a board in his red flannel pajamas. Beside me, tears streamed down Sandy's cheeks. Her eyes were squeezed shut. No tears came from me, but I dug my nails into my hands. No one spoke as we drove down the freeway.

Eventually we reached the sanitarium, which was a brick and plastered building. Mother went ahead of Sandy and me, holding Daddy's hand, as we walked up the steps of a front portico supported by high columns and stopped at a massive door. I didn't want it to open and swallow up my Daddy. But Mother picked up the brass knocker and banged it down.

At the sound, the door opened. A tall, slightly bald man in some kind of uniform asked, "How can I help you?"

"We have an appointment to see Dr. White."

"Oh yes. We are expecting you. Please follow me into the waiting room."

Daddy started to walk away. Mother said sharply, "Edgar, take my hand."

He knotted his fists, the blood vessels on his temple increasing in size, but he allowed Mother to lead him through the lobby into the receiving room. Once we stepped into the office, my father pounded the walls with his fists. As Sandy and I stood watching in horror, a doctor in a white coat and two other assistants rushed in, restrained my father, and led him down the hall.

A receptionist handed Mother some paperwork to fill out. "You'll need to fill these out before you leave."

While Mother filled out the papers, Sandy and I sat next to the wall in two straight-backed wooden chairs. My throat felt closed up so that I couldn't swallow. *My nightmares are real. Daddy frightens me.*

CHAPTER NINE

PRESENCE

Don't be afraid and don't panic, for I, the Lord your
God, am with you in all you do.

—Joshua 1:9

As we drove home, Mother sat rigidly behind the
steering wheel without a glance in our direction
or words of comfort. Sandy sat next to her in the
passenger seat. I sat in the back seat, feeling
shrunken in size and very alone. I had a taste of blood in my
mouth from biting my lips. Stony silence like a tomb filled
the car all the way home. But once again, by the time we
arrived home, I'd managed to banish my feelings of terror by
disappearing into my mind and disassociating from my
surroundings.

This time, Daddy was gone several months. Without his
peacemaking, emotions flared. Sandy picked on me. Mother
yelled. I whimpered. Then Mother left to be with her mother
again, leaving us with her friends, the Fletchers, for several

days. I felt like a discarded rag. Nor was this the only time. Sporadically, whenever my father was gone, Mother would just pack up and leave to our grandmother's home, leaving us with the Fletchers. Once again, she never explained why she didn't take us along. Perhaps she really was concerned that we not miss school. But it felt as though she just didn't want us around.

At other times, one of my father's older sisters, Aunt Ortha, came to stay with us. Aunt Ortha was married with a daughter, but since she was older than my father, and he in turn had been in his thirties when I was born, her daughter was grown and gone before I had opportunity to really know her.

Aunt Ortha herself was hunched over with short, permed gray hair, and her manner towards Sandy and me was stoic and unfriendly. She also had a nervous tick that made me uncomfortable. I had never been a bed wetter since I'd become toilet trained as a toddler. But whether my anxiety over my mother's absence or the apprehension I always felt around Aunt Ortha, something triggered a bed-wetting episode while she was there. To punish me, Aunt Ortha washed my mouth out with soap.

It never occurred to me this was unkind and cruel. I just blamed myself. I must be no good for her to do this to me. To give my mother credit on this occasion at least, she was furious when she found out about the soap upon her return.

My father's entire family lived right in La Mesa, but we didn't have much of a relationship with them either. My grandfather was a candy-maker and had a store where he sold his homemade candies along with magazines, newspapers, and other odds and ends. I remember occasionally being taken to the store, where he would give me a piece of candy. But like my mother's parents, he never visited us, and certainly we spent no holiday occasions together.

The one member of my father's family we saw on any regular basis was his other sister, my Aunt Margaret, who lived quite close by. She was married to my Uncle Jack, but she had no children of her own, and at least while I was still a small child, she pampered and cossetted me, buying me beautiful picture books and letting me come over to spend the night. Experiencing some semblance of motherly affection brought such a joy to my little heart. She would powder me up with fragrant-smelling talcum powder, let me crawl into her high poster bed, and read to me or play card games.

All this helped distract me from the dark cloud that resided in my home and my heart. I focused instead on the pleasantries of my life—nature, friends, games, play. Once again, disassociation helped me deal with the pain. But I could no longer concentrate well on the teacher's instructions. I, who'd been an A student, now kept my head down, trying to avoid the teacher's eyes. She often gave me a puzzled look when I didn't respond. I in turn felt embarrassed, stupid, and out of touch.

"Sue is a nut," I doodled on my school papers.

My friends didn't seem to notice that I was in a stupor much of the time during class. Being a natural chatterbox, always eager for a smile or encouraging word, I shifted gears as soon as my feet hit the outdoors, turning into the life of the party once I was skipping and running with my friends.

But once I got home to our two-story house, all sunshine felt blocked out. And not just because our curtains were always drawn shut. The house felt empty, not lived in.

Mother continued to disappear behind the closed door of her bedroom. I didn't know then, and in fact would not find out until well into my adulthood, but my mother suffered from an obsessive-compulsive anxiety disorder, for which she would eventually be diagnosed.

But at the time, all Sandy and I knew was that our mother's housekeeping practices were extreme and certainly not normal in comparison to what we saw at our friends' homes. Along with keeping blinds and doors closed on even the hottest days to seal out air and light, she'd hang up magazines to air out before reading them so as to avoid toxins. She was afraid to open the refrigerator door for fear of a cold draft. She'd often wear a mask in the house for fear of germs. Even the spotlessness of our home was more of a manic constant cleaning than a reasonable standard of hygiene. We never had visitors to my recollection to brighten up the doom, and other than the Fletchers, my mother appeared to have no friends.

Sandy coped by staying away from home. Or maybe she was back in her hideaway under the house. I didn't bother to find out. I felt detached, dumb, my feelings banished far from my mind. Not to be noticed. Not important. Not to be bothered with.

When I came home, I would throw my school papers and lunch pail down on the kitchen counter and head outdoors. We had not gone to church again after those few visits during kindergarten. Still, the beauty of God's creation spoke to me time and again of His presence. The scent of sagebrush rising from the canyon down below permeated the air. While I knew only that its scent was heavenly, I learned years later that sagebrush has healing properties and is used as an antioxidant, to stabilize metabolism, promote better brain function, and to treat anxiety. Maybe that's why I felt so much better after spending time there.

Our passion flower vine on the northern side of our garage fascinated me too as I examined its intricate parts. Its blue and white flowers, about two inches across, formed an intricate pattern of leaves, tendrils, petals, and filaments. The flower was named after the Passion of the Christ, as its various parts were believed to symbolize the sword that pierced Jesus' side, the whips that struck Him, the crown of thorns placed on His head, and the Holy Grail, respectively.

So God spoke to me through Nature, in a code expressing His beautiful handiwork. But though I embraced Nature's beauty and found it a comfort, my heart was heavy. I missed Daddy. By now he'd been gone two months. Somehow, the days slipped by, running into one another.

Then one morning as I was getting ready for school, the phone rang. I could hear my mother's voice, high-pitched and excited. "Edgar can come home today? We'll be there in the afternoon, after the kids get home from school."

My heart beat with eager anticipation as Sandy and I skipped to school. When I told my friends that my father was coming home, I was bombarded with questions. "Was he sick? Where was he? How long was he gone?"

My eyes welled up in tears, but I smiled, "He's been in a hospital, but he's okay now."

After school, Mother, Sandy and I piled in the car, windows down, fresh air massaging our faces, as we drove to the sanitarium. This time it didn't look like such a frightening place bent on swallowing up my Daddy. This time it was going to open its doors and release Daddy, all healed.

Walking quickly to the columned portico, we all knocked on the massive front door. The man who opened it smiled and gave Mother a hearty handshake. "Glad to see you. Edgar is ready to go home. Follow me."

He led us down a long hall with few lights. It seemed darkly oppressive. Behind several closed doors, we could hear loud, agonized screams. I stiffened, suddenly engulfed with emotion. But Sandy grabbed my hand. "It's going to be okay. Daddy's coming home."

Daddy's room was at the end of the hall. Mother, a worried look on her face, hesitated before knocking softly on the door. We heard loud, racing footsteps. Then Daddy threw open the door open. With unrestrained joy, he picked Sandy and me up, swinging us back and forth, saying how much he missed us, how much he loved us.

He then gave Mother a kiss such as I'd never seen before. Mother seemed a little stiff and uncomfortable, but from her expression, I think she liked it. Bliss filled my heart as we walked down the hall as one united family. We piled into the car, Daddy behind the wheel, one arm around Mother, scooting her closer to him. Sandy and I sat in the back seat, nudging each other and raising our eyebrows up and down. I felt secure, comfy.

Mother turned the radio on, shifting through the channels until she found the song, *You are my Sunshine.* We hummed along with the lyrics. "You are my sunshine, my only sunshine. You make me happy when skies are grey. You never know, dear, how much I love you. Please don't take my sunshine away."

Then Daddy announced, "They just advertised the Barnum and Bailey Circus is coming to town. Do you want to go?"

Sandy and I exclaimed, "Yes!"

Mother remained motionless, quiet.

I leaned over the front seat. "Don't you want to go, Mother?"

"We'll see."

I sat back into my seat, wondering why Mother didn't want to join us. That night, I walked into the den, as we called the room where we had our TV and spent leisure time. There I caught Daddy and Mother sitting on the couch, bodies touching, embracing one another. They looked up when they saw me, grinning from ear to ear. Seeing their happiness together filled me with joy.

A few days later, the day of the circus arrived. I changed into my favorite red polka-dotted blouse and blue pants, then thumbed through my drawer for a blue bow Daddy had bought me. I felt pretty as I clipped the bow to the left side of my long blonde hair. Sandy wore a red plaid shirt and red shorts, her long brown hair tied back into a pony tail.

Racing for the car, we both jumped in the backseat. Daddy sat behind the steering wheel. He looked healthy and happy, his green eyes dancing. Mother stood next to the car, her arms folded across her chest. A shadow crossed over Daddy's face. "Are you sure you don't want to go?"

"No, I'm tired. I don't feel well." She looked pale, eyes downcast.

Daddy shook his head. "That's too bad. You're going to miss a lot of fun. We'll be back in a few hours."

Some of my own happiness evaporated. *Why isn't Mother happy? Daddy's home. Doesn't she like us?*

I climbed into the front seat next to Daddy. Sandy stayed in the back seat. Daddy inserted the key in the ignition, and off we went. We pulled into a parking lot next to a large tent. Sandy and I grabbed Daddy's hands, pulling him towards the entrance. Inside, vendors walked by, yelling, "Ice cream! Sodas! Cotton candy!"

I tugged at my father's hand. "Daddy, Daddy. I'm hungry. Will you buy me something?"

Cotton candy in one hand and a soda in the other, I followed my father and Sandy up the steep bleacher steps. We found three empty seats in the center back. My heart beat fast as I looked down at the clowns, tigers, and elephants. A man walked on a tight-wire high above my head. Trapeze artists flew through the air, turning somersaults.

"Daddy, how come they don't fall?" I asked.

"They've worked hard, hours every day. Practice makes perfect," he said with a chuckle as he poked both of us. "Just think what you two could do if you worked hard."

"Really," Sandy answered. "I'd like to work with animals, maybe be a doctor."

"What about you, Sue?"

"I don't know. I'm not smart like Sandy."

"That's not true," Daddy said.

On the way home, Daddy told us about the elephants— that they have a good memory, sleep standing up, and talk to each other in their own language.

"What about the tigers?" Sandy asked.

"They are cats, the largest of their kind. But the cheetahs run faster. They can run as fast as a car."

CHAPTER TEN

TROUBLED WATERS

The raging of the sea; when the waves thereof arise,
you still them.

—Psalm 89:9

Our fun lasted this time for quite a long period. I loved being around Daddy. He was smart and took us places. And he always had time for me. We played ball on the front yard and ping-pong in the garage. He would run around the back yard with me on the top of his shoulders. Or wrestle me to the ground and tickle me into hysterics.

When I heard the ice cream truck playing its minstrel music, I would dash into the house, knowing Daddy would give me money for a purchase. He also gave me money to buy candy at our local store. My favorites were chocolate Necco wafers, Life Savers, and candy cigarettes. These last were reflection of the times, since smoking had not yet been deemed unhealthy, nor was making a candy version so children could pretend to smoke considered inappropriate.

In contrast, Mother didn't join in our fun and seemed almost nonexistent in our lives, disappearing into the shadows. Sandy, Daddy, and I tried to please her and include her in our fun. But she always declined without an excuse and seemed encased in a dismal world of her own. I learned to rely on Daddy for my needs.

With the consistency of Daddy being home, my listening skills improved, bringing good marks at school and praise from the teacher. But in the middle of my third-grade year, Mother dropped a bomb that exploded in my mind. She told Sandy and me to watch Daddy's eyes. That wide-eyed, blank stare such as had frightened us in the past would be signal of another breakdown.

The thought terrified me. I didn't dare look at Daddy for fear of what I might see. Would he be changed again into someone I didn't recognize or know? Would he hurt me? Would he leave us again? If I did glance up at him, I could see that his green eyes were once again opened too wide, staring in space. He didn't say much, nor did I. Was he going to be sent away again?

My mind pushed such thoughts away, clinging to the positives in my life—food, a roof over my head, my friends, the outside rustle of leaves, the wind in my hair, the songs of birds. But just two weeks later, I was in the den, absorbed in a comic book where Donald Duck had moved into a house that wasn't his and discovered a diary about a gentleman burglar.

I was turning the page when I heard Daddy ranting and raving loudly. Dropping my comic book, I opened the door into the hall. There I saw him chasing my screaming mother down the hall, his fists clenched. Mother dashed into the bathroom and slammed the door in his face. As Daddy pounded on the door, yelling at her to open it, I ran from the den into my bedroom, where I hid under my bed.

Sometime later, I heard Mother on the phone with Mr. Goodman. "Can you come over? Edgar is having another mental breakdown. You have a way of calming him down."

Eventually, the front door opened. I could hear Mr. Goodman's voice. Then Daddy's yelling ceased. Mother called out, "Sandy, Sue, get ready to leave."I dashed out of my bedroom and into the kitchen. Daddy was still there, drinking a beer, but Mr. Goodman had left. "What's going on?"

"Mr. Goodman thinks we should take your father to the desert for a change of scenery," Mother explained. "Hurry up and help me pack our trailer."

My parents owned an Airstream camping trailer that sat parked in an empty lot next door. I had no memory of actually going anywhere with it or even having stepped foot inside it, though Sandy used to sneak inside to smoke cigarettes there safely out of reach. Following Mother's orders, Sandy and I helped load up some travel essentials. Then we climbed into the back seat of Daddy's Oldsmobile while Daddy silently hitched the trailer to the back of the car.

Mother looked worried as she stood watching Daddy, her hands on her hips. "Edgar. I'll drive."

Nodding, Daddy climbed into the front passenger seat. Mother put the key in the ignition, gripped the wheel, and we drove eastward toward the Anza Borrego Desert, which was about a two-hour drive from San Diego. I stared out the window at a sky that suddenly looked gloomy. The trees along the roadside looked twisted, lifeless. We finally turned onto a dirt road, gravel tossed up under our car fender sounding amplified until we came to a screeching stop.

"We're here," Mother announced.

We had arrived at Anza Borrego Desert State Park. Climbing out of the car, I walked into hot, dry air that tasted like dirt. Daddy was already unhitching the trailer. I glanced at him out of the corner of my eye. He had a slight smile on his face, so I heaved a sigh of relief and followed him into the trailer. Rays of sunlight through its small windows revealed the sleeping quarters at the rear, a tiny kitchen, an eating area, and a small bathroom.

Sandy and I helped Mother put away some of the belongings we'd brought along. Daddy grabbed a beer out of the ice box. Taking a big gulp, he opened the door, looked outside, and said with enthusiasm, "Hey, before the sun goes down, let's take a walk." I looked up at him, afraid of what I might see. But his green eyes were dancing in merriment. Taking hold of Daddy's good humor, all four of us stepped out into a dry stretch of barren sand. Beyond the camping ground with its spaces for trailers and tents was the open desert. As we walked, Mother pointed out small desert flowers and told us their names. Daddy showed us a barrel cactus and explained how they store water. Sandy and I chased lizards that darted into our path.

"What's that?" Sandy pointed. "I see something moving up there on that hillside."

"Bighorn sheep," Daddy said. "They are the animal for which the Anza Borrego desert is most famous."

Sandy and I raced toward the bighorn sheep, but they leapt over rocks and ran off into the distance. Clambering up the hillside, we were still trying to spot them again when the sun began to slump over the horizon. The sky lit up in brilliant colors of yellow, orange and red. We returned to the trailer as one happy family—at least on the outside.

Mother cooked hamburger patties. Sandy helped with the salad. I set the table. We sat as a family, but unlike our desert hike, Daddy was now once again unusually quiet. Tension filled the air. After dinner, Mother, Sandy, and I cleaned the kitchen and finished unpacking. Daddy remained seated, staring into space.

Wanting to help, I looked around for something, anything, that might distract him. I spotted a deck of cards on our kitchen shelf. Daddy had played canasta with us in the past. Maybe he would play now. Grabbing the deck of cards, I took a seat next to him. "Daddy, do you want to play cards?"

He just sat there wide-eyed with a blank look. Then he knotted his hands together. His feet slammed down on the floor as he jumped up. The trailer's single small closet had a full-length mirror on the door. Racing over to it, Daddy started yelling incoherently at his image as though at an imaginary enemy. I stood horrified, speechless.

Taking a step back, Mother put her hand on her heart. "Don't worry, he won't hurt you."

But my very next memory was waking up to Mother screaming. Looking into the kitchen, I saw Daddy's hands covered with blood. "What happened, Mother?"

Mother grabbed Sandy and me, pulling us out of the trailer and into a nearby shed used as storage by the campground. "Stay in here. Don't come out. I'm going to try to find a telephone to call the police."

But Sandy and I snuck out as soon as she left. We immediately spotted Daddy in the dirt road, trying to flag down one of the cars going past. Finally, a car pulled over. Daddy jumped in and punched the driver. I blanked out. My next memory was seeing Daddy sitting in a car, exposing himself.

"Mother," I yelled, horrified, covering my face with my hands. "What is Daddy doing?"

By now a police car was speeding up the campground road. As its brakes screeched, several uniformed policemen threw the cars door open and raced towards Daddy. When he resisted, they held his hands down and forced him into the backseat of the police car. As they carted my daddy off to the sanitarium, Mother drove Sandy and me home in stony silence. I sat rigid with shock, my breathing shallow and my hands cold and clammy, but without releasing a single tear.

The next morning was a school day, but I couldn't get out of bed. My mind was spinning, my throat closed up so I couldn't swallow. Mother allowed me to stay home from school. I stayed in bed, immobile, staring into space like Daddy.

"What's wrong with me?" I managed to ask my mother.

"You're going to be fine," she replied. Then she shut the door and left.

CHAPTER ELEVEN

RECOVERY

Do not be afraid—I will save you. I have called you
by name—you are mine.

—Isaiah 43:1

Two days later, my resilient spirit kicked in, my fears tucked away behind closed doors in my mind. I dressed, ate breakfast, then headed out the door to school. Nature greeted me with a slight breeze shifting through the full pepper trees that lined our street. My best friend, Flora Lou, who lived across the street, joined me for the walk to school.

"Where have you been?" she asked with a grin.

I smiled back. "Oh, I just didn't feel well."

As I entered our classroom, Mrs. Glasgow, my third-grade teacher, rose from her desk and walked to the front of the class. "Today we'll begin a new book, *My Father's Dragon*. It's about a young boy who rescues a baby dragon Sue, will you help me pass out the books?"

83

"Oh, yes!" Feeling special, needed, I hurried to the front of the class and picked up a stack of books on the shelf behind the teacher's desk. The cover showed a boy hugging a large yellow-and-blue-striped dragon. I couldn't wait to start reading it. Mrs. Glasgow passed out math sheets next. I inhaled deeply, enjoying the pleasant odor of the solvent mixture used to make copies in the ditto machine.

After school, I headed to Flora Lou's house. Both her parents worked, her father a policeman and her mother a school principal, so I spent a lot of after-school hours at her house. We would raid the cupboards for food, use her bed as a trampoline, and have pillow fights. She taught me how to do yo-yo tricks, including "rock the baby" and "walk the dog", and we played canasta for hours. I was known as an excellent card player, mainly because I thought nothing of cheating by drawing too many cards in my hand or discarding extra cards I didn't want. In fact, I'd become expert enough that Aunt Margaret would invite me over to play with her friends. When I won, they would shower approval on me, which made me practically burst in pride. Of course, neither my aunt nor her friend knew I was cheating.

But my friendship with Flora Lou was short-lived. Sandy resented that we were friends. They had been friends first, and Flora Lou was actually closer in age to Sandy, who was now eleven, than to me, an eight-year-old. For revenge, Sandy kept a pail of water on our balcony and dumped it on Flora Lou's head when she came over to play with me.

Flora Lou ran home crying and didn't come back for days. But that wasn't enough. Sandy defecated on Flora Lou's front porch. When Flora Lou and I walked together going to and from school, Sandy would cut in and shove Flora Lou aside.

She even called Flora Lou's house, threatening to beat my friend over the head with a baseball bat.

To make matters worse, Flora Lou and I found the jar in which Sandy had stashed her Halloween candy haul, which for some reason she kept in a kitchen cupboard instead of in her room or some hiding place out of our reach. Opening the jar, we stuffed our mouths full of tootsie rolls and jelly beans. We were just putting the jar away when we heard Sandy entering the house. Leaving the wrappers behind, we ran into my bedroom and hid under the bed. It wasn't long before she discovered our theft.

"Sue, you've been in my candy jar!" Sandy yelled. "Where are you?"

Stomping into my bedroom, Sandy looked under my bed, discovering Flora Lou and me underneath. Flora Lou let out a squeal. I froze. Lifting up the bedspread, Sandy dragged Flora Lou out by her feet, pulled her into an upright position, and slapped her face.

"Your face is getting nice and red. I need to match the other side." As she slapped Flora Lou on the other side of her face, I crawled out from under the bed, horrified and afraid of my mean sister. Flora Lou ran home. Her parents called our home, complaining about Sandy's behavior.

"Yes, this is Sandy's mother," I heard my mother respond. "She did what to Flora Lou? Oh I'm so sorry. I'll see that she's punished."

As far as I knew, Sandy was never punished. But Mother's growing dislike for Sandy was becoming apparent. She often told me, "You're growing faster than Sandy. When you're tall enough, you can beat her up."

Mother was never consistent with her favoritism, but just why she disliked Sandy so much was a mystery to me. One explanation was even more bizarre than the symptoms she displayed of her obsessive-compulsive disorder. When my sister was born, Sandy had been red and wrinkled, as of course most babies are. Mother insisted that her newborn baby looked just like the devil. She even threw out all Sandy's baby pictures.

In fact, she kept only a handful of pictures of either Sandy and me, none at all from our infancy. The only picture I remember of my own childhood showed me as a toddler of perhaps two to three years old. In any case, during this particular period, Mother showed a clear preference for me, calling me pet and treating Sandy as though she didn't belong in the house.

At other times, it was the other way around. Mother ignored me and only talked to Sandy. She would tell Sandy repeatedly in my presence how smart she was and that I was only average.

As might be expected, Sandy felt Mother's rejection. It was from a dark shadow in her own heart that she picked on my friends. She'd ask their height, then say, "I didn't know shit could grow that tall." They would eventually just leave my house, never to return. I didn't want to beat my sister up, but I was afraid of her, so I just kept my distance and avoided catching her eye.

Mother often dropped us off at Knott's Berry Farm on her way to visit my father at Norwalk Sanitarium. This was a huge park filled with rides, shops, and restaurants. At only eleven and eight years old, Sandy and I were both afraid at being left there on our own. Clasping each other tightly by the hand, we would venture forward into the crowd of strangers. We'd fill up on cotton candy and coke, then ride the park train over and over again. At least for a while, bound together in our mutual need, we would act like sisters again.

But once we were back home, I rarely saw Mother or Sandy. The house felt swallowed up in loneliness and insecurity. As always, the outdoors became my escape. One of my favorite outside games was to bounce a tennis ball off the side of the house. One day after Sandy had turned twelve, I was bouncing the ball forty times in succession when I heard Sandy inside crying. I froze, stunned. Crying was avoided in our home as a sign of craziness and a lack of control.

Rushing into the house, I found Sandy and Mother in the kitchen. Mother had the phone pinned to her ear, her expression angry as she said, "Thanks for taking Sandy in. I can't control her, and with Edgar gone, she's just too much."

Sobbing, Sandy wrapped her arms around Mother's waist and pleaded desperately. "I don't want to move in with Aunt Margaret. What have I done wrong? Why do I have to go? How long do I have to stay?"

Mother pried Sandy's arms off her waist. "You're too hard to manage."

I didn't want Sandy to leave. Although she was mean to my friends, she wasn't to me. In fact, when she'd caught me in tears trying to do a book report, she'd offered to help. I pressed my lips together in a tight line as I thought back to the times Mother dropped us off at the Fletcher's for several days to go be with her mother. *Mother doesn't like us. She doesn't want us around!*

And, now at just twelve years old, my sister was being kicked out of the house! Why! Sure, Sandy had snuck out at night a few times to be with her friends, smoked on a few occasions, and stolen things once in a while. But Mother had never reprimanded her, whether Mother didn't know or just didn't care. So long as Sandy kept her bedroom clean, helped in the kitchen, pulled weeds in the yard, and generally stayed out of the way, Mother gave her no notice. So why would Mother do such a thing as sending my sister away from her own home? And what about me? I tried to please Mother too. Would I be next?

Anxiety with its claw-like fingers now encircled and swallowed my home. Mother took on a job as secretary for a nearby school and rented out Sandy's upstairs spare room. Strangers now lived in my house, used the same kitchen, sat in the same living room, walked down the same hall, went up the same stairs. Mother was gone all day at work, leaving me alone to face my fears.

When darkness fell, and I retreated to my bedroom, my fears escalated to an overwhelming terror. My breath came out in gasps when the outside door that lead to my bedroom creaked open in the middle of the night. Could it be one of the boarders? The oleander tree scraped against my window on a windy night, sounding as though someone was trying to get in. Once again, I escaped through dissociation, sealing my fears away from my conscious self. What a relief to wake up and find the sun's rays shining through my bedroom window. I'd made it through one more night!

Going home after school was just as difficult. When the school day ended at 2:30 p.m., a knot formed in my stomach. I counted each step with dread. Once I arrived home, I'd grab a quick snack and head back outdoors. Pulling an orange from one of our fruit trees, I'd scramble down the embankment into the canyon. Only when I reached that refuge would my fears turn into courage. I didn't leave the canyon until the sun was low in the sky, which told me that Mother would be home from work.

"Mother. I don't like strangers in my house," I told my mother. "They might hurt me."

She just shook her head. "They're fine. Just ignore them."

Once again shoving my fears behind the closed doors of my mind, I'd spend the evenings watching television by myself in the den until Mother yelled from another room, "It's time for you to go to bed."

Even safely in bed with the door closed behind me, I was assailed by the creaks in our new house, tree branches rubbing against my window, howling wind, thunder, and lightning during storms. I would bury myself in the blankets like a mole, gasping for air, feeling defenseless with no place to turn. Daddy was gone. Sandy was gone. Mother didn't offer care or protection.

Still, I hadn't forgotten completely those few Sunday school lessons before we'd moved or that there was a God who loved children and promised to protect them. When I was most afraid, I would ask God for His protection and to bring my Daddy home. When I finished praying, a wave of peace would sweep over me, and I just knew Daddy would come home.

Daddy did come home a few weeks later, but not the way I expected. In the middle of the night, he barged into my bedroom, leaned over, and held me tight. In between sobs, he repeated, "I love you. I love you."

I froze, paralyzed in fear. But almost immediately, police officers were rushing into my bedroom, and pulling Daddy away from me. He fought against them, his eyes red and blazing with fury. Putting him in a choke hold, they forced him out of the house and drove him back to the sanitarium from which he'd escaped.

My mother was pacing back and forth next to my bed. I asked her, "Mother, what happened to Daddy?"

Her face was pinched in a frown. "He's considered dangerous. He will now have to be locked up."

Terror now filled me to the breaking point. Digging my nails into my hands, biting my lower lip, I fought for control. I didn't want to go to a sanitarium like Daddy. So I forced my feelings into check without shedding a single tear. When morning came, I dressed for school as usual in a bright yellow dress. As I ate my breakfast, Mother was at the counter with her back to me, making peanut butter sandwiches for my lunch.

"Why did Daddy act like that?" I asked. "Do you think he would hurt me?"

Mother didn't turn her head to look at me. "It's best if we don't talk about it."

At that point, dissociation took over. I sat in school that day with my mind blanked in shock, anxiously chewing my pencil and deaf to the teacher's instructions. Yet when the recess bell rang, I jumped up with a smile on my face. As we played on the monkey bars and swings, I laughed with my friends. Nobody knew what was happening inside me or saw any difference—not even me.

CHAPTER TWELVE

A TIGHT GRIP

For God gave us a spirit not of fear but of power and
love and self-control.

—2 Timothy 1:7

On my tenth birthday, Mother bought me red
lacy baby-doll pajamas. I wore them in the den
while escaping into my favorite television
programs. There were the Eastside Kids, who
confronted various stock villains. Charlie Chan, a benevolent
detective, who solved mysterious crimes. And the witty
Groucho Marx, who hosted a question-and-answer game
show.

As I was watching TV, one of the current renters joined me
in the den. He had a round belly like a bowling ball, gray,
bushy eyebrows, and a split between stained teeth. Pulling
me close to him, he put my hand into his pants. When my
hands felt wet. I thought he'd urinated and calmly got up to
wash my hands. Under complete control, I matter-of-factly

told a friend, who in turn told her mother. Her mother must have told mine, since Mother kicked the renter out.

Not long afterwards, I returned home from my usual escape into the canyon to find another strange man in the kitchen. As I stood, speechless, he gave me a broad smile. "You must be Sue. I'm happy to meet you. I just bought some donuts. Would you like one?"

Avoiding his eyes, I walked over to a box of donuts on the kitchen table.

"What kind would you like?" he asked. "My favorite is the strawberry cake donuts."

This time I did look at him. "Chocolate, thanks."

The new renter was pleasant to look at with blue eyes that sparkled and deep dimples. In a short time, I'd latched onto him as a friend. He played catch with me in the back yard, read my favorite book *Heidi* to me over and over again, and looked through my school papers with interest.

Sometimes he read magazines in our living room. One day as I passed through, I glanced at his magazine. "What are you looking at?"

"I'm a nudist. My magazine shows pictures of my nudist colony, what they do, how they live."

"Can I see?"

He handed me the magazine. I flipped through the pages in shock and fascination. They contained scenes of nude people eating their meals, playing volleyball, cards, horseshoes. What fun it must be not having to wear clothes. Then a thought struck me. If my friend was a nudist, perhaps I could see his nude body.

"I've never seen a man without clothes before," I commented.

"Would you like to see me?" he responded.

For a minute, I didn't say anything. When I finally nodded, he went on, "We'll have to plan a time and place. What time does your mother get home from work?"

"She comes home around 4:00. I'm home from school by 2:30."

"Okay. Let's meet tomorrow at 3:00. Knock on my bedroom door. I'll open it in the nude."

My heart fluttered in anticipation. The next day, the clock on the wall in my classroom ticked away the minutes with excruciating slowness. When the dismissal bell finally rang, I took off in a sprint. But by the time I arrived home, enthusiasm had turned to apprehension.

I told him I wanted to do this, I reassured myself. I have to follow through. He's expecting me. He won't hurt me. He's nice.

It was a few minutes after 2:30 p.m. when I walked into the house. Taking off my school dress, I put on my favorite red blouse and plaid shorts, grabbed a Mighty Mouse comic book off my bedroom shelf, and went into the den. My attention wandered as I turned the pages. Tick, tick, tick went the den clock. When it read 2:55 p.m., I headed upstairs and tapped on my grown-up friend's door. I heard footsteps inside approaching the door. "Who's there?"

"Sue," I said in a whisper.

"Are you ready to open the door?" he asked in a gentle voice.

"Yes." I opened the door a crack and peeked into the room.

He stood in front of me, wearing a black and red striped robe. "Are you ready?"

When I nodded, he released his sash, slipped the robe off his shoulders, and unabashedly allowed it to drop to the floor. I gawked for a split second, then looked away. A moment of silence passed as I shifted my weight and shuffled my feet. Then I asked, "Do you want to see my body too?"

"No," he responded with a slight chuckle.

I walked away unharmed, satisfied. That was the last encounter I remember with him. But there were plenty of others renting the upstairs bedroom. I treaded carefully with watchful eyes, wondering who would be the next interloper in my home. Then one night, Mother was in the kitchen, preparing supper.

"Sue, help me set the table," she said.

I was setting out her brown placemats when I felt something dark, evil, behind me. Turning around, I saw another strange man staring at me. This time his black gaze felt sinister, filling me with terror. Grabbing at my mother, I whispered. "That man scares me. Please make him leave."

Of course, she didn't. After that encounter, I began having nightmares of being underground in a dark place where people dressed in black cloaks were chanting and large wooden crosses were burning. In my nightmares, I was placed in a coffin, naked. Mother was there too, red faced, eyes filled with piercing hate, cackling as if demented.

But as usual, I pushed the nightmares down into the dark recesses of my mind and focused intentionally on my blessings—a roof over my head, food on the table, friends to play with, and the sweet sounds and melodies of nature. My encounters with the ominous roomer were closed in a sealed compartment of my mind.

By this point, Sandy had been living with Aunt Margaret for two years. But when her husband, our uncle, became gravely ill, she was told she'd have to leave. Mother accepted Sandy moving back in with a restrained hug and tight smile. But I was happy to see her. Following her upstairs to her bedroom, I sat on her bed and watched her unpack her belongings: a few long pants, eight shirts, and several dresses. Her two pairs of shoes were put in the closet. She looked glum.

"Are you glad you're home?" I asked.

She frowned. "Yeah, but I think our aunt cares more about me than Mother."

"Mother doesn't care about me either," I said glumly.

"She didn't kick you out of the house!" Sandy retorted.

I let out a deep breath. "I wish I could sleep upstairs with you. I've been having bad nightmares. We used to have such fun, sharing the same bedroom, even the same bed. Remember the made-up stories we told under the blankets?"

Sandy shrugged, her face expressionless. Didn't she want to share her bedroom with me? Maybe she didn't like me either. After a strained silence, she said, "Ask Mother."

I ran downstairs. "Mother, can I sleep upstairs with Sandy?"

"No," she responded shortly.

"Why?"

"Because."

My shoulders drooped. *She hates me*, I told myself.

Early the next morning, the phone rang. Then I heard Mother saying, "Oh, I'm so sorry. What did he die of?"

I rushed into the kitchen. Mother was standing by the telephone with her hand on her forehead. "What happened?"

"Uncle Jack just died. Pneumonia."

When Sandy heard the news, she covered her face with her hands and sobbed. Hands on her hips, Mother frowned at her. "Stop crying like that. You have no reason to be so upset."

I was shocked. How could Mother be so mean and heartless? After all, Aunt Margaret and Uncle Jack had been Sandy's family for the past two years. I bit my lower lip. *She doesn't like me either.*

Uncle Jack's death settled the question of Sandy going back to Aunt Margaret's home. The next morning, Mother explained what would be our duties from then on. "Sandy, you're going to be the outside girl. You do the yard work. Suzie, you're the house girl. You clean the house."

Sandy's eyes flashed with anger. "You don't want me in the house. You just want to get rid of me, not see me."

"That's not true," Mother insisted. But Sandy gave me a fierce look. Did she blame me for Mother's decision? I had nothing to do with it!

There turned out to be a reasonable basis for Mother's decision on our chore assignments, which if she'd pointed out kindly, might have assuaged Sandy's feelings and improved the relationship between Sandy and me. Sandy was gifted with a green thumb. She could nurse plants back to health and would bring seedlings in from around the neighborhood to grow in our garden. Even at that young age, she could discuss knowledgeably about grafting, mulching, and other gardening terminology that to me were mysteries. Under her care, our yard flourished.

But as far as Sandy and me, it seemed to us both that Mother actually encouraged sibling rivalry. Sometimes Mother would call me her pet. Other times she ignored me and only gave Sandy attention. This fostered walls of separateness between my sister and me. Sandy began giving me dreadful looks. My body tingled with fear whenever she picked up the grill off the stove, lifting it high above her head and threatening to hit me with it. She never carried out her threats, but once again I was learning to keep my distance from her.

She would often sneak around so Mother and I didn't see her. Once I caught her behind a bush watching Mother and me taking clean clothes off the line. When she gave me the middle finger, I felt a rush of fear, but turned my attention to the sweet, fresh scent of clean clothes as Mother and I folded them into a laundry basket. *The heck with my sister!*

A smile crept onto Mother's face as we both picked up the laundry basket and walked up the back steps into the house. "You are my pet again this week, Suzie."

My eyes lowered as we placed the basket next to the linen closet. "Mother, why can't you just treat us equally?"

Ignoring me, she began putting some towels away. But the very next day, Mother looked me up and down. "You're ten years old. Sandy is thirteen. I don't think you're going to be taller than Sandy. Why don't you beat her up now?"

Following her orders, I marched through the house. I found Sandy in the washroom at the back of the house, hand-washing some of her clothes. Ignoring the hammering of my heart against my chest, I doubled up my fist and hit her on the back with all my might. Sandy turned around in complete shock and disbelief. I too was stunned, suddenly afraid of what I had done.

At that point, I noticed an empty milk bottle out in the hallway just inside the back door. In that time period, milk bottles were not disposables, but made of a thick glass. The milkman would set the bottles of fresh milk ordered by each household just inside the back door and pick up any empty bottles left there to be refilled.

Snatching up the empty bottle from its place by the back door, I stepped back into the wash room and threw it at Sandy. It hit Sandy's foot. I don't remember if the bottle actually broke, but it did draw blood. Sandy screamed, "I'm going to get you for this. Just you wait!"

For some time afterwards, Sandy limped. I wasn't worried about her tattling to Mother, since Mother was the one who'd egged me on to fight Sandy. But I was certainly scared of what Sandy might do to get revenge. I did my best to stay away from her, leaving early in the morning and making sure I didn't get home until after Mother returned from work. Sandy never did take any specific revenge, other than returning to her prior methods of tormenting me.

By this point, the only time Mother, Sandy, and I spent together was at dinner. Sandy and I would sit stiffly at the kitchen table, avoiding each other's eyes. Mother kept her back to us, eating on a chopping board at the kitchen counter. Once dinner ended, Sandy and I would pick up our dishes and head for the sink. In silence, she would wash while I dried. After we finished our duties, Mother and Sandy would go upstairs into their own bedrooms, not to be seen until the next morning.

Television kept me company. Roy Rodgers and Dale Evans became my dream parents. Roy Rodgers was handsome, had well-defined features, a good build, and a happy twinkle in his eyes. Dale Evans was beautiful with long, dark wavy hair and a smile that lit up her face. They were a happy couple who showed mutual respect and trust for each other, a contrast to my "real" parents.

They also protected the helpless, raced down dusty roads chasing bad guys, and fought with six-shooters on their hips. The program over, I would hum their theme song, "Happy Trails Again", as I headed for bed. Nightmares still woke me up on occasion, leaving me feeling as though I were falling into a dark pit with no escape. But once again I remembered those early Sunday school lessons and reached my thoughts out to God. He at least was always there and never left me.

Chapter Thirteen

God's Messenger

The Lord is good to those who wait for him, to the soul who seeks him.

—Lamentations 3:25

T he air was gentle and the sun shining as I stepped outside to hear a familiar tune floating in the air. I looked over our back-yard fence. Mrs. Graham, our neighbor, was pounding in a garden trellis stake while humming the tune, "*Happy Trails Again.*"

"Hey," I called out, leaning over the fence. "You're humming my favorite song. Do you watch the *Roy Rogers Show*?"

Mrs. Graham took off her straw hat, displaying a gray bun, and smiled at me. "Every week. Their theme song plays over and over in my mind."

"Me too! And I love your flowers."

"They're called dahlias," she explained. "Would you like to come over and pick a few?"

"Okay, sure." Hopping over the fence into her back yard, I looked around at a rainbow of flowers. "Wow, these are so pretty. And big! Those there must be a foot across."

"You're exactly right," Mrs. Graham responded with a chuckle. "Dahlias can grow to twelve inches across easy. That's why these big ones are called 'dinner plates'. You know, God designed these flowers. He is the Creator of all good things."

I knew that much about God from those long-ago Sunday school lessons. I picked a few red and white dahlias. Then she gave me a hug. "Come over any time you want."

When I got home, I put the dahlias in a vase on my bedroom dresser, gently rubbing my fingers over their soft velvety petals. Then I lay on the bed, gazing at the flowers. *Mrs. Graham says God created all good things. God created me, and I don't feel good. Could God make me as good and beautiful as these flowers?*

A few days later, I was outside in the back yard when the smell of cookies baking wafted my direction from Mrs. Graham's house. Walking over to our shared wooden fence, I saw Mrs. Graham opening her screen door to step outside.

"Hi," I called. "Are you making cookies?"

She turned in my direction. "Oh, hi there. Why yes, I am. I just took a batch out of the oven. Why don't you come over and try one?"

"Sure. Thanks." I hopped over the fence and headed across her yard. Mrs. Graham ushered me to a chair at her kitchen table and set still-warm cookies on a small plate in front of me. Munching one, I looked out her window. "Look, there's a bird outside at your bird feeder. It has red on its breast. What kind of bird is that?"

"It's a house finch." Mrs. Graham was pouring milk into a glass. "Would you like some milk with your cookies?"

"Sure, thanks." As I washed down the cookies with gulps of milk, Mrs. Graham made friendly conversation. "How's school? What subject do you like best? Do you have a favorite friend?" At some point, she slipped in, "Do you know God?"

"I don't know much," I told her. "My family doesn't go to church. But when I feel sad or scared, I pray to God."

"Good." Mrs. Graham placed her hand over her heart as she added, "God hears all our prayers."

Mrs. Graham's home became my refuge. Her kind, caring words soothed my troubled soul. Her faith in God gave me assurance of God's love and protection.

Around this same time, I made a new friend named Deneen, who was in my fifth-grade class. She had long, blond curls, a pug nose, and a real family—mother, father, and two sisters—who laughed together and shared easy conversation. Although I felt out of place, they accepted me as part of the family, and I spent every moment I could at their house. We'd often gather around the television set, eating buttered popcorn and watching my heroes, Superman and Roy Rodgers, come alive on the screen.

One day after school, as Deneen and I were walking to her house, I said to her, "Hey, Deneen. I know an easy way to make money."

"How?"

"Let's go door to door, collecting money for a church."

"Do you think we should?" she asked doubtfully. But when I urged her, she agreed to help. Arm in arm, we walked up to doors and knocked. The people who answered the door believed our story about collecting for a local church, and we ended up with as much as two dollars in change in one day, which was a nice sum of money in the 1950s. With no qualms of conscience, we would spend our loot at the Five and Dime Store, buying games, candy, or ice cream. Sometimes we even went to the movies.

This wasn't the only delinquent behavior I was displaying. Sometimes for kicks, I would walk by a mailbox and toss a lit match inside. I felt no twinge of conscience, just fun for the moment. Deneen and I also began setting fires in trash cans we found in an alley or in bathrooms. The bright colors dancing around brought instant gratification.

It might seem odd, but I didn't really feel I was being a bad person. To me, being good was obeying my mother—doing my house work, not talking back, staying out of her way. Beyond that, I had no real code of conduct, which can be attributed largely to the fact that I'd never been taught one. My father was gone too much to do so. My mother never got involved in my behavior or Sandy's so long as we were compliant in dealing with her.

All this began to seriously impact my conduct at school. My mind elsewhere, I had a hard time focusing on the teacher's words, which made me feel stupid. One day while I was sitting in my classroom, reading a book about the Civil War, a tall, slender woman wearing a crisp white blouse and blue skirt entered the classroom and walked up to my teacher, who was sitting at her desk. A moment later, my teacher looked over at me. "Sue, you need to go to the office."

My school book dropped out of my hands, a sinking feeling squeezing at my stomach as I rose to suddenly shaky legs. Had someone found out I'd been stealing money and setting fires? Was I going to be kicked out of school? If so, what would my mother do? Would she even care? What if Daddy found out?

But the woman in white and blue led me right past the principal's office and into the nurse's office. By now, I was confused. *I'm not sick! What's going on?*

"Sue, sit down on this chair," the woman told me. "Your teacher thinks you may have a hearing problem, so we're going to check your hearing."

I let out a deep breath of relief. Having my hearing checked was a whole lot better than everything else I'd been imagining. The woman hooked me up to a machine and put huge ear muffs on my ears. "Raise your hand if you hear a sound."

As each sound came through the ear muffs, I raised my hand high. At last, she took off the ear muffs and smiled. "Finished. You did quite well. The problem is clearly not your hearing."

As the woman led me back to my classroom, my mind felt fuzzy. The teacher was now explaining plant ecosystems, but I couldn't focus on what she was saying. Digging my nails into the palms of my hand, I scolded myself sternly. *I've got to start listening! My friend Sally flunked last year. I don't want that to happen to me! So far, I've passed all the tests. But can I keep it up, or am I going to flunk?*

I managed to graduate into the sixth grade. My delinquent streak also graduated to a higher level. Deneen and I no longer left the house without matches, ready for another exciting blaze. After all, a few fires weren't hurting anybody, were they? Stealing from a church and lighting fires wasn't my own bad behavior. At some point, I discovered a jar of coins in our den closet. I'd grab a handful of coins and use them to buy donuts at a little store across the street from the school. Again, I felt no guilt.

In the midst of my unnoticed delinquent behavior, Daddy finally came home. It had been two years since I saw him. When he stepped through the front door, I felt a lump in my throat. He looked older, thinner, tired. But when he broke out in a smile and his green eyes danced, my misgivings vanished. This was my handsome Daddy home again.

After dinner, Daddy said, "Let's go outside for a walk. I've been cooped up so long."

Mother shook her head. "I'm glad you're home, but I'm not up to a walk tonight. Maybe tomorrow night."

Daddy's smile immediately turned to a frown. My chest ached. Mother made Daddy unhappy. *Why can't she join us? Doesn't she like Daddy? Does she like me?*

Leaving Mother behind, the rest of us stepped outside into warm, balmy air that rustled the pepper tree leaves lining our street. Sandy pointed at the night sky. "Daddy, look at all the stars out tonight. They look like cut glass."

Daddy's green eyes lit up like the stars. "How many stars do you think we can see?"

I jumped up and down. "A thousand million."

"No," Sandy corrected me. "I read in school it's only thousands."

"Well, you're right, Sandy," Daddy grinned. "We can see only about five thousand, but there are billions out there."

"Wow," I exclaimed. "Do you think people live out there?"

"Not on the stars," Daddy said. "They're just hot gas. Maybe on a planet like ours."

Sometime shortly after Daddy's return, he suggested, "Hey, why don't we take a trip to a tourmaline mine. We'll discover beautiful pink jewels hidden inside ordinary stones."

"Can we really go, Daddy?" I said. "Will Mother come?"

Daddy winced. "I'll ask her."

Mother refused to come, but within a week, Daddy, Sandy, and I were driving north from San Diego, chatting merrily. When we reached our destination, Sandy and I raced into the open plain where rocks were laying in waiting for hidden discoveries.

"Daddy," I asked. "Are there really pink stones hidden in these rocks?"

"I wouldn't kid you, would I?" Daddy pointed to a small storefront where a sign announced: "Mining tools here."

Hammers and chisels in hand, we cracked open rocks, uncovering beautiful pink stones hidden inside. As we drove home from the mine, I sat next to Daddy, my heart filled with love. Even tired and thin, he was so handsome compared to other girls' fathers I'd seen. He was smart too. He'd taught me how ants carry fifty times their weight, birds migrate thousands of miles, and bees dance to show where they found nectar or pollen.

So why did he have to get sick and leave us? What had made him the way he was? Maybe it went back to his own childhood. I didn't know much about it, but I'd heard enough stories over the years to know that Daddy never had it easy. He was the youngest of the three siblings, as well as the only boy, and his mother had died when he was still quite young. Though he was highly intelligent, successful, and popular in high school, his home life had been much less happy, his relationship with his father a deeply troubled one. By the time Daddy reached his teens, his father was routinely kicking him out of the house in a rage. He would throw Daddy's belongings, packed up into a suitcase, out onto the street. Retrieving them, Daddy would walk a few blocks to stay with his grandmother.

Did his own unhappy childhood and the trauma of parental rejection plant the seeds of his later mental illness? We would never know. But one result of the abuse he received from my grandfather was that Daddy bent over backwards to be a kinder, more loving, caring, and giving father to Sandy and me than his father had been to him.

Well, at least I did have a mother, unlike Daddy. Although Mother never hugged or kissed me, she'd once told me I was good down deep. That I could get along with anyone. I took a deep breath, stuck my head out of the car window, and enjoyed the wind buffeting my face.

CHAPTER FOURTEEN

DISCIPLINE

Folly is bound up in the heart of a child, but the rod of discipline will drive it far away.

—Proverbs 22:15

Although Daddy was home, my delinquent behavior continued unchecked. I began ran-sacking through magazine stands outside store fronts to steal sexy magazines and sneak them home. Why not? I wasn't hurting anyone. My favorites were *Young Romance* and *Real Love*. I knew Sandy hid dirty books in the attic next to her bedroom. Following her lead, I found my own place to hide them in the attic.

But the law finally caught up with Deneen and me. Not over the magazines, but a trash can we'd lit on fire in an alley. Unbeknownst to us, the fire had spread to a wooden fence next to the trash can. We were sauntering down the street when we heard an approaching police siren. That was when we realized we could smell smoke.

We dashed to hide behind a large trash bin, but it was too late. The police car had stopped, and a moment later, the officer strode up to us, legs apart, arms crossed. "Did you set a fire in a trash can?"

When we didn't answer, he ordered us to get into the police car. We sat in the back seat, crouched down like ashamed criminals. Once the officer found out where I lived, he drove me home. I shook with silent sobs as he gripped my arm and marched me up to my front door. At his pounding knock, Daddy came to the door. He looked shocked and speechless as the officer explained my criminal behavior.

"I am so sorry," Daddy told the officer. "Be sure I will mete out the appropriate punishment."

Expecting the worst, I felt my face twist in anguish as Daddy led me into the den with a heavy frown. But instead of punishing me, he simply sat down with me on the couch and dropped his face into his palms. "This is my fault. I haven't been a good father. I haven't been home enough."

A tidal wave of shame flooded me at his words. I never did receive any punishment, but I also never set another fire. All went well until several weeks after his return, Daddy realized there were coins missing from a collection he'd kept hidden away in a jar in the den closet. He immediately knew who was to blame. Seeking me out, he demanded bluntly, "I'm missing some coins. Have you been taking them?"

I nodded slowly, looking at my feet. His eyes blazed. "Those were valuable, old coins. Why would you do this?"

"I didn't know they were old coins. I just wanted to buy donuts with my friends. I'm so sorry! I won't do it again." Shoulders slumped in guilt, I headed to my bedroom and flopped face-down on my bed, trying to hold back the tears. *How could I do this to Daddy? He looked so hurt, so sad!* I never stole another of his coins.

Even though I was embarrassed and ashamed at being caught, I felt a certain relief at having a parent actually express concern and even disappointment over my behavior. So long as Sandy and I didn't cause her any trouble, Mother never seemed to care what we did, including delinquent acts like stealing, setting fires, or smoking. Daddy's own problems made it impossible for him to really deal with my issues or Sandy's, but at least he took an interest and handled it the best he could.

Daddy had now been home six months. Strangers weren't living in the house any more. My sister was home too. We all shared the same dinner table, though Mother always looked grim and Daddy was silent. Still, Daddy went to work and came home on schedule. Since he had a successful law partner who'd kept their business going, he'd been able to step back into a thriving practice.

Still, if on paper we once again showed the makings of the American dream family, real life was far different. Daddy and Mother avoided spending time together. Mother removed herself from any emotional attachment to Sandy and me. Sandy made herself invisible. With my anguish tucked inside, I tried to pick up the pieces. Be helpful. Be cheerful. Make a difference. Find love. Acceptance. But our house was an unhappy, gloomy place. I felt to blame. No matter how I tried, I couldn't make a difference.

Friends became my lifeline. Sometime in seventh grade, Deneen and I had a big fight, splitting as friends without a backwards glance. Aunt Margaret had stopped inviting me over and made it clear she didn't want me around anymore. Since I'd always bent over backwards to be polite and sweet to her, I didn't understand her changed attitude. I came to the conclusion she just liked cute, little girls, not big, adolescent ones like me. Either way, from that point on, she always treated me with contempt, her language towards me on the rare occasions we still visited being mean and sarcastic. Not that she treated Sandy any better.

Mrs. Graham was still my neighbor, but I'd grown out of spending time at her house, so even that comforting friendship was gone. I was feeling at loose ends for companionship when I began noticing several other girls my age walking to school together. They looked like a rough bunch, but by this point I was desperate for friends, and just about anyone would qualify.

Vivian had long, dark hair, large teeth, and looked ready to punch life in the nose. Barbara had blonde hair and a constant sneer. Kathy was the prettiest one with rounded cheek bones, a slim nose, and high brows. They were not nice or kind girls. They would walk down the sidewalk with their middle finger sticking straight up. They swore, and when they passed little kids playing outside, they threatened to beat them up.

Still, I was desperate enough for friends that I was soon hanging out with them, laughing with them and participating in their bad behavior. This included smoking. When they offered me a cigarette, I readily accepted. In no time at all, I was blowing out smoke rings with the best of them. I began stealing my father's cigarettes, which I would take to school and smoke in the school bathrooms.

One day after school, Vivian suggested, "Let's go to North Park and see who can steal the most."

"Sure!" we all chimed in.

North Park was a shopping area filled with stores and boutiques. Once we arrived there, we split up, each stole as much as we could, then met a couple of hours later to go over the loot. I puffed up with pride as my friends oohed and ahead over my stash of clothing, jewelry, and makeup.

From then on, I couldn't go into a store without looking around for the opportunity to steal. I figured the stores had plenty of merchandise. I needed it more than they did. And it was so easy! Just like cheating at cards. Walk in and case the joint. When no one is looking, stuff your bag, pockets, or purse, put stolen goods under your top, then glance around to make sure no one noticed and calmly walk out.

My reward was having a full wardrobe of up-to-the-minute clothes instead of Sandy's hand-me-downs or the Salvation Army thrift store clothes Mother bought me that were often faded, not the right size, or just plain ugly.

Just don't get caught! remained my motto. But some of my classmates knew. They would point their fingers at me and announce, "She's wearing stolen clothes."

Again, I had no conscience over any of my behavior. I would ask classmates to look at pictures in their wallets, then steal their money. Of course, I denied it when they accused me of stealing, since I knew they couldn't prove it. Plus, I figured I needed it more than they did.

The kids at school passed out slam books, a 1950s version of Facebook, where they would write comments under a different student's name on each page. Comments on me included: "She's full of shit . . . Haven't had the pleasure to meet her, if she is one . . . Ugly is as ugly does, and she's ugly."

My already fragile self-esteem fell to a new low. I was wretched, a mess through and through. Then Daddy noticed my extended wardrobe and marched into my closet to investigate. Seeing stacks of clothes on my closet shelf, he stomped into the kitchen, where I was eating a snack. "Sue, where did you get all those clothes?"

Startled, I choked on my cookie. "What clothes?"

"The ones in your closet. Come with me." Marching me into my bedroom, he pointed to my stolen stash, his eyes blazing.

"Where did these come from?" he repeated.

I shrugged. "From a friend."

"Which friend?"

He promptly called up several friends, who denied giving me the clothes. Daddy's face turned red, the muscles in his jaw clenching. "Either you stole the money from me, or you stole the clothes from stores. I hope you stole the money from me."

Once he coerced the truth from me, Daddy promptly took me to each of the stores where I'd shoplifted. "I am a lawyer. My daughter has something to say."

By the time I'd finished confessing, I felt sick with remorse. *I've probably ruined Daddy's law practice! Who would want to go to him with a criminal daughter like me?* As with the fires and coin thefts, I was overcome with guilt and shame—not at my transgressions themselves, but at Daddy's disappointment in me—to the point that my stealing came to a screeching halt.

Daddy forgave me, as he always did. Once again, he was the one who took time to play catch with me on the front lawn, his eyes sparkling and his laughter easy. Or ping-pong in the garage, which he would let me win. We went horse-back riding in the country and ate our favorite ice creams bars together, mine chocolate and his vanilla.

Then one special Sunday morning arrived. As we were eating our breakfast of eggs, bacon and potatoes, Daddy announced with his green eyes dancing, "Change your clothes after breakfast. We're going to the Laguna Mountains. I have a surprise for you."

After breakfast, we all piled into the car, Sandy and I in the back seat, Mother and Daddy in the front, and headed eastward toward the Laguna Mountains, which were about eighty miles inland from the Pacific coast. The narrow road climbed steeply around hairpin turns high into the craggy mountains. Looking down at forest and meadow below, I asked, "Daddy, how far up are we?"

"Six-thousand feet. Higher than a mile. We'll be at the summit soon. That's where your surprise is." Gravel hit our bumper as Daddy made a sharp right turn onto a dirt road. We drove up to a small log cabin nestled in oak trees.

"Wow, is this ours?" Sandy asked.

Daddy's smile was wide and beaming smile. "You bet! It's going to be our vacation home."

"Are we rich?" I demanded.

Daddy chuckled. "The law practice is doing okay."

We all stood outside the cabin door while Daddy pulled a key from his pocket and inserted it into the key hole. Inside, the cabin had two bedrooms, a small bathroom, and a high-beamed living room with a large rock fireplace. The kitchen was outfitted with modern cooking appliances.

Sandy and I headed out the back door where we saw a large shade tree with an undergrowth of ground ivy. We were exploring the cabin grounds when I heard Mother and Daddy arguing. I stopped cold, holding my breath as I listened.

"I can't come out here," Mother was saying angrily. "I'm going to have allergies with all that dirt and pollen."

Then I heard the front door slam, and Daddy called, "Come on, girls. We have to leave."

Decayed tree leaves crunched under my shoes as I headed unwillingly towards the car. *Mother doesn't have allergies,* I said to myself as I slid into the back seat. *She just doesn't want us to have any fun.*

The car engine sounded to me like an angry beast as we sped back westward. As soon as we arrived back home, Sandy disappeared from sight. My soul felt scrubbed by a wire brush as I looked up at Daddy's glum face. When Mother headed upstairs to their bedroom, Daddy followed, shutting the bedroom door behind them with a bang. Creeping upstairs, I put my ear to their door to eavesdrop.

"Jane," I heard Daddy give an exasperated puff. "We need to have more family fun. But I can't get you to leave the house. You say you have allergies, but I've never noticed you even with a sniffle. And though we have enough money, every time I tell you to buy some new clothes, you decline my offer. I don't know what to do to make you happy."

Mother blew her nose. "You don't care. I'm very sensitive to germs and the outside air."

I stopped eavesdropping and headed back downstairs. I don't know how to make mother happy either. I do my chores without complaint. Don't talk back. But she still doesn't like me.

CHAPTER FIFTEEN

PERSEVERANCE

You need to persevere so that when you have done the will of God, you will receive what he has promised.

—Hebrews 10:36

From then on, I frequently heard yelling upstairs. My troubled mind reeled with questions. Were my parents going to get divorced? Was Daddy going to have another breakdown? Bang the walls? Chase mother down the hall? Be taken away from us? Would strangers move back in?

Once again, I pushed down my pain and tears. I became numb. When I looked in the mirror, what I saw—blonde hair, little brown eyes, a fat face—seemed unappealing, unlikeable, even ugly. Once again, I was having a hard time listening or concentrating in school, and my grades fell. Going home was another dread I couldn't avoid. One day I arrived from school to find Daddy with his pajamas still on, unshaved, leaning over a cup of black coffee at the kitchen table.

"Daddy, didn't you go to work?" I asked worriedly.

He inhaled deeply. "No Susie. I wasn't up to it. Go along. I'll be okay." But he didn't look okay. As before other breakdowns, his eyes showed too much white.

Sometimes I went through the cupboards. Pulling out sugar, flour, butter, and nuts, I made batches of homemade cookies and ate them all myself. Food provided a source of instant gratification. I binged on weekends, my stomach swelling like a balloon.

In the mornings, I would wake up worried that Daddy was no longer home and go charging upstairs to my parents' bedroom door, not relaxing until I heard Daddy breathing heavily, still sound asleep. Or I would sit outside on the curb in front of my house, not wanting to go in. Our home looked so good on the outside, one of the nicest in the neighborhood. But inside it was a house of torment, where a beam of light hardly dared peep through the drawn curtains, and few visitors ever crossed the threshold.

Sandy coped by staying out of the house as much as possible. I in turn just ignored my feelings, tucking them deep inside. I was determined to appear normal. Carry on. Survive.

Then one day after school, Sandy greeted me with impish glee, grabbing me by the arm. "I feel like taking a walk. Do you want to go down the canyon together? I have something to show you."

I was surprised, but happy my sister wanted to be with me. We headed out the backyard and down the embankment. Once we reached the bottom of the canyon, Sandy stopped at a tall tree and pointed to a little platform on the top.

"Climb up there," she said with a snicker. "Something's waiting for you."

I climbed up, scratching my legs in my hurry, but not caring in my excitement to see what my surprise was. But when I got to the platform, I stared in disgust. It was a pile of poop, already covered with flies! "Sandy! That's terrible. How did you get it up here?"

She clapped her hands with a slight smile on her face. "Wouldn't you like to know."

I pinched my nose. "Why do you poop like this, even on Flora Lou's doorstep?"

"It's a gift, directly from me."

Covering my nose, I crawled down and ran toward the stream below. Sandy followed me yelling, "It doesn't hurt anyone. I think it's funny."

Our lack of any normal code of conduct was very apparent. But so long as she, like I, was respectful to Mother and did our duties without complaint, Mother left us alone on any decisions, needs, and bad behavior that didn't affect her.

I was inured enough to Sandy's behavior that I'd erased the image and smell from my mind by the time I climbed down from the tree. I sat down next to the rushing stream. The sweet aroma of blue and yellow wild flowers filled my nostrils, and birds sang sweet melodies. Then Sandy plopped down next to me and stretched out her legs. "Have you seen Daddy lately?"

Her question burst my momentary bubble of contentment. Trapped-up worries spilled out of my mouth. "Not very often. And when I see him, he doesn't look like himself. Do you think he's going to have another breakdown?"

Sandy's eyes looked like a pulled-down shade. "I don't know. Mother's no help. All she says is to watch his eyes." She tugged at her hair. "Let's go home."

We arrived home to find Mother lying down in her bedroom upstairs, covers over her head. Though Daddy should have been home from work by now, there was no sign of him. Sandy tapped Mother on her shoulder through the covers.

She stirred, "Do you want something?"

My voice trembled. "Where's Daddy? Did he leave us again?"

She pulled down the covers to look at us with fevered eyes. "He's back in the sanitarium."

"How come you didn't tell us?" Sandy asked.

Mother struggled for breath. "I didn't want to upset you. The doctor said they had some medication that might help. He should be home within the week. Now, would you two please leave? I think I'm going to have an asthma attack."

Sandy's footsteps could be heard bolting down the stairs, but I stood frozen, staring down at my mother. With a voice that cracked, I asked, "Can I help?"

"Yes, would you bring me a glass of water?"

I galloped down the stairs, anxious to bring a smile to her face. When I returned with the water, she just turned her head away from me. "Thanks."

Setting the water on her bedside table, I went back downstairs, lifting one heavy foot after the other, and fell face down on my bed. A gallon of tears lay trapped under my eyes. A voice deep inside wanted to cry out, but couldn't. Over the following weeks, I felt swallowed up into a dark pit of torment. Yet no one seemed to notice, certainly not Mother or Sandy. They were each bearing their own pain. They rarely talked to me and showed no signs of caring how I felt.

Alone in my misery, I dissociated again, sealing my emotional trauma into a locked chamber, away from my conscious self in order to maintain order within and without. Still, however unhappy I felt inside, my outward demeanor continued to show a smiling face. I didn't dare allow myself to feel and express my emotions, lest I be locked up like my father. I reconnected with my tough friends, but they just taunted me and called me a sissy for no longer stealing with them or joining in their cursing. They even threatened to beat me up.

It wasn't a week as Mother had promised. But a few weeks later, Daddy did return home again, acting ready to greet the world and me with outstretched arms and warm kisses. Although Mother looked at him with suspicion and turned stiff when he hugged her, my heart bubbled over in happiness that Daddy was back. My past terror and anguish was safely locked away. My life switched in high gear.

As my father opened the back door, ready to depart for work, I asked, "Daddy, is it hard to come home, go back to work, just like nothing happened?"

He picked me up and twirled me around. "No, my partner and trusted college friend keeps our law practice alive, and I know you're happy to see me."

Although Daddy was home and back to his old self, I carried within me a dark place—a sense of shame for my broken family and a sadness for my mother, whom no one could please. I lived in a constant state of perplexity, often taking my seat in the wrong desk at school. When I realized what I'd done, I'd hang my head in embarrassment, feeling even more stupid. I tried not to hear snickering around me as I stumbled toward my own seat and plopped down, avoiding any eye contact.

Mother added to my low self-esteem, telling me several times that my sister was the smartest person she ever knew, while I was "average" quality. She suggested I should become a teacher, as that was a career for students who couldn't do anything else. Conversely, she spoke of Sandy as though assuming she would graduate from the University of California at Berkeley, as she and Daddy had. I kept an appearance of normalcy plastered on my face while self-disgust was growing inside.

CHAPTER SIXTEEN

GOD'S LEADING

Does not he see my ways and number all my steps.
—Job 31:4

T hen another bomb dropped to explode in my face. Just as had happened the prior year, in the middle of class the door opened and a stern-looking woman marched up to the teacher, this time in a black suit. After a short discussion, the teacher looked over at me. "Sue, you need to go to the principal's office."

My heart thudded against my chest. Last time it had turned out to be just a hearing test, but maybe this time I really was in trouble. Did they know I smoked in the bathroom and stole magazines? As I followed the woman into the principal's office, I was horrified to see Daddy and a counselor waiting for me. Somehow, my limp legs carried me to the nearest chair.

The principal sat straight, stiff, and strong. "Sue, we're going to transfer you from Wilson Junior High to Roosevelt Junior High."

My face felt frozen, my mouth wide open. How could they make such a drastic decision without even consulting me? "Why? What have I done wrong?"

"The friends you've been hanging around with are a bad influence on you," the principal said. "A fresh start will do you good."

What did any of these people know about my friends, or what I was doing? Certainly, neither Mother nor Daddy had shown any interest in what friends I had. And they had no idea of all the wrongs I'd done. But I didn't voice my objections, since clearly no one cared to listen to them.

I looked over at Daddy. He looked glum, but was nodding in agreement. As Daddy and I left the office, he put his arm around me. "It's going to be for the best."

The night before I started my new school, Daddy took Mother, Sandy and me out to a choice restaurant. Candles flickered on the tables. The noise of people talking, laughing, clinking their glasses in good cheer, filled the air. Their mouths were moving too quickly, their movements too fast. My body felt detached, my mind dull.

"Sue, you can order the most expensive meal on the menu," Daddy said with a smile.

My feelings clearly weren't important to him. I thrust another layer of pain and anger behind locked doors of my mind as I ordered a steak dinner.

The next morning came, the clouds hung low, the sky as gloomy as I felt. Daddy patted me on the shoulder. "It's going to be fine. Just wait and see."

As we drove west toward Roosevelt Junior High School, my body felt like a mannequin, a shell of a real person. My hands, folded in my lap, felt like they weren't mine.

Daddy leaned over towards me. "Susie, are you okay. You haven't said a word."

"I . . . I didn't hear you," I stammered.

"I asked how you were. Your eyes look glazed over."

"I'm okay."

Daddy parked the car outside the large building that was my new school. "I know this is hard on you, but it's for the best."

I rubbed my eyes hard. "Why? What did I do that was so wrong, to be kicked out of school?"

My father remained silent as he led me up the steps and to the school office. I looked down at my feet, wanting to crawl under the counter, while he spoke to the receptionist. "This is my daughter Sue. She is transferring from Wilson Junior High."

"Why yes. We were expecting you." The receptionist offered me an outstretched hand. "Welcome to our school. You'll like it here."

I looked away, ignoring her outstretched hand. Coming to her rescue, my father shook her hand instead. Then an office monitor, slender with a full head of long, blonde hair and hot pink lipstick, appeared. "Hi, Sue, I'll take you to your new classroom."

We walked down a long hall, passing classrooms of chattering kids who all knew each other. I felt friendless, shy, self-conscious. When we reached my new classroom, the office monitor walked me up to the front of the class and introduced me to the teacher. "Mrs. Blackwood, this is Sue. She's going to join your class."

Mrs. Blackwood shook my hand with a warm smile. "So nice to meet you."

Maybe this isn't going to be so bad after all, I thought. But when I saw the other kids staring at me, my soul shriveled. I'd gained a good bit of weight that past year through my binging on cookies and other goodies. So much that my mother had added to my already poor self-image by dubbing me "tire-tube tummy". Now it felt like these kids were all taking in every extra pound. With my head down, I worked my way back to the desk I'd been assigned and plopped down in my seat.

The bell shrilled, announcing school had begun. Mrs. Blackwood took her place in front of the class. "We have a new student. Her name is Sue."

As dozens of heads swiveled to look me up and down, I felt lightheaded and squeezed my own eyes shut to block out my fear. The teacher's voice sounded indistinct, hard to hear, as she began her lecture on the latest scientific discoveries.

When the lunch bell rang, the other students poured out to take their seats at the lunch tables, talking, laughing, and sharing their food. Finding a seat, I ate my lunch alone. By end of the day, I was anxious to go home and hide under my bed covers. It was a longer walk home than my prior school. As I arrived out of breath, the phone rang. When I picked it up, a gruff voice said, "Is this Sue?"

"Who is this?" I demanded.

"This is Vivian. We found out you switched schools. You think you're too good for us. But just watch out. We're going to find you and beat the shit out of you."

Sandy walked into the kitchen just when I hung up the receiver. Seeing my lip trembling, she asked, "What's wrong?"

"Some kids from Wilson said they were going to beat the shit out of me."

Sandy knotted her fists. "Not if I get to them first."

Sandy was tough, yet beautiful and smart. I was proud of her and happy she was my sister, who stuck up for me if I was in trouble. Still, she was in high school, while I was in junior high, so how could she help me? Daddy had given me a ride that first day, but now I had to ride the bus or walk, which meant I'd be alone and unprotected.

The next morning, my heart was beating hard against my chest as I headed to school. My eyes darted left and right, every shadow a possible threat. But I saw no sign of Vivian and her friends. When school was over, I rushed into the bathroom and hid until I was sure Vivian would no longer be lying in wait for me and I could head home safely. I continued doing this every afternoon until one day some of the other girls noticed.

"What are you doing in here?" they asked. I felt so embarrassed and ashamed that I just sprinted for home, wrapped up in a cocoon of insecurity and self-hate. During the following weeks, I was once again completely out of it—a zombie case. Through inattention, I misplaced my purse, wallet, and jackets. I daydreamed instead of listening to the teacher. My voice came out with a stutter.

One day when I was daydreaming through a lecture on biology, I was called into the counseling office. The counselor was a middle-aged woman with short, permed hair and a probing gaze. I didn't care for her from the start. But for the next month, I had to see her weekly. She would lean forward, hands on her lap, and wait for me to initiate the conversation. I felt put on the spot, restless, and uncomfortable. How could I convince her I didn't need help? Maybe if I lied to her about how much I enjoyed school and that I'd work hard to improve my grades.

That worked, and I didn't have to see her again. As the weeks went by with no bodily harm from Vivian and her pals, I stopped hiding in the bathroom. Mother bought me a bus pass so that I didn't have to walk all the way home. I made a few friends who walked to the bus stop with me.

Then one day a girl with tousled brown hair blowing around a freckled face approached me. "Hey, I've noticed we go home the same way. My name is Charlene. Where do you live? We could be neighbors."

We discovered we lived only a few blocks apart and soon became good friends. She had pool parties and would invite Louise, June, and Lyla, classmates who also became my buddies. My self-hate and weak confidence softened when they gave me a smile of approval.

One day Charlene asked me, "Sue, how come you don't smile?"

"Because I look ugly when I smile."

"No you don't. You have a pretty smile. And you're cute. You just need a bit of a makeover." Charlene taught me to curl my eyelashes, wear pink lipstick, and fix my hair in the current fashionable hairstyle. Maybe I wasn't so ugly, I decided. With improved self-confidence, my stuttering disappeared. I dieted and felt more comfortable with my body shape.

Louise, June, and Lyla added another dimension to my growth and development. Lyla was a natural beauty with long, curly hair, large blue eyes, a perfectly-formed little nose, and a small cupid mouth. Easy-going and friendly, she gave a lot of parties, always including me. Every weekend I walked two miles to her house, where we would share tea with milk and sugar in the kitchen or sit on her bedroom carpet listening to popular songs like *Rock Around the Clock, Diana,* and *All Shook Up.*

Louise came to Lyla's house too. She was the darling of the school—cute with a turned-up nose, full lips, green eyes, and a perfectly oval shaped face—so I was thrilled just to be in the same room with her. We didn't talk much. I didn't feel worthy. Besides, Lyla was the talkative one who filled in any silences with her chatter.

But one day Louise and I happened to leave Lyla's house at the same time.

"Hey, would you like to come over to my house?" Louise asked.

Me, the ugly, stuttering newcomer of the group? My heart thudded at the thought, but I managed to stammer, "Sure, th-thanks."

Louise's mother, wearing an apron over a flowered housedress, greeted me as soon as we walked through the back door. "You must be Sue. Louise told me about you. So glad to meet you. I just finished making some cookies. Help yourself."

A flood of happiness filled me as Louise and I grabbed a handful of warm chocolate cookies and went upstairs into her bedroom. It was large and beautiful—a room for a princess. See-through lace curtains draped her large windows. Sprays of vine wallpaper covered her walls. Delicate doilies dressed her end tables.

"Let's sit on the bed." Louise puffed up a pillow and sprawled out on top of her white chenille bedspread. I followed her lead. Our conversation flowed comfortably, easy and relaxed. She made me feel safe, no longer afraid of attack or ridicule. From then on, I spent many nights at her house. We discussed fears, insecurities, friends, school, and misdeeds. The subject of my own family life was never brought up.

On one special over-night stay, we were in the kitchen, where her mother was washing the dishes, when Louise announced, "I've found my best friend ever!"

If I'd had buttons on, they would have busted off. Wow! She valued me as much as I valued her. Later, we were eating some scones her mother had made when Louise asked, "Sue, do you believe in God?"

I brushed crumbs from my hand. "I'm not sure what I believe. I went to church a few times with my parents. I've even prayed when

I needed help. One of my neighbors, Mrs. Graham, believes in God and talks about Him sometimes. But how can I know if there really is a God? Or if He hears my prayers? And if He does hear, does He even care about me?"

Louise's eyes were lit from inside. "Sue, you need to believe in God. He is your Father in heaven. He doesn't just care about you. He loves you."

In that instant, God transformed Louise into His divine messenger. Her hands folded in her lap as she tilted her head upward in prayer, she seemed to me an angel looking up into another dimension, a golden glow surrounding her. She spoke no further words on the subject to me, nor needed to. For that moment at least, her faith became mine. I felt I could fall over her balcony and a loving Father in heaven would catch me. I would hold that memory close to my heart as my journey in life continued.

CHAPTER SEVENTEEN

PATIENCE

The Lord works out everything to its proper end.
—Proverbs 16:4

June was another of Charlene's friends who became my good friend as well. With her flawless reddish-blonde page-boy haircut, large, blue eyes, and white-toothed smile, June was the glamour queen of the school. She was also well-known and admired for being San Diego's "Little Miss Sunbeam Bread", Sunbeam being the bread company that sponsored the popular *Time for Beany Show*. June planned on being a movie star and told me she'd welcome me into her mansion when she became famous and rich.

I was impressed, imagining June's future stately home with three stories, ten bedrooms, and an indoor pool. But besides her beauty and potential riches and fame, June was smart, a deep thinker. Together we would analyze the meaning of life, how we fit into the grand scheme of things, or what we might become later in life. She made me feel intelligent, someone worthwhile talking to.

My days still began in a dark place, dreading to get out of bed and face the world. But thanks to my new friends, once my feet hit the ground, I actually found myself looking forward to school and seeing my friends. Lyla, the bubbling-over free spirit of fun. Louise, the sensitive and caring one. June, the intelligent beauty queen. And Charlene my surrogate mother. Together, they made me feel I wasn't such a worthless person after all.

But even with my improved self-esteem, Mother could always pull me back down into self-hate. One day I was combing my long, blonde hair in my bedroom mirror, feeling quite satisfied with my upturned nose and light-brown eyes, when Mother walked into my bedroom. Looking me up and down, she said with a frown of disapproval, "You're sure not sexy!"

Her words were like a bucket of ice water poured over my good spirits. *She's right!* I agreed, frowning at my image in the mirror as my mother left the room. *I am ugly. I'm not worthy of feeling good about myself.* And one more layer of self-hate drove away my momentary feeling of confidence.

By now Daddy had been home close to a year. My parents' relationship seemed increasingly strained. Mother had no interest in joining Sandy and me when Daddy took us horse-back riding, drove us to carnivals and fairs, or played catch with us on the front lawn. And Daddy himself was often absent for meals. One morning, I'd gone into the kitchen to get a glass of water when I overheard Mother and Daddy screaming at each other in the den.

"I've put up with you twenty-three years," Mother snarled at my father. "I can't stand it anymore. You have to leave."

Sure enough, a few months later, I had to go to court in the middle of my math class to testify in their divorce hearing. I did so emotionlessly as though it were no big deal. And to me, that is how it seemed. After the divorce, Daddy and Sandy moved in with Aunt Margaret, who had lived alone since Uncle Jack died and welcomed the company.

I stayed with Mother, who began renting the spare room again, this time to women. Strange women who looked like gypsies, read tarot cards, and gave out fortunes. They avoided me, and I avoided them, spending most of my time with my friends. The rest of junior high slipped by on an even keel. After Daddy divorced my mother, he seemed like his old happy self. Sometime later when I was a sophomore in high school, Daddy invited me out to lunch. His voice was animated, so I knew something was up.

We ordered barbequed pork sandwiches. While we waited, Daddy leaned over and squeezed my hand. "Suzie, I have a question for you. Your Aunt Margaret introduced me to a lovely woman. I want to marry her. But if you disapprove, I won't."

"Oh, Daddy. I want you to. You deserve some happiness."

"Thanks for your permission. I wouldn't have married if you didn't approve."

I felt like doing cartwheels and jumping jacks between the tables. Daddy cares about me! He values my opinion! He consulted me before making an important decision!

Sandy was less excited than I about Daddy's remarriage. At the time I didn't understand why she would get so emotional over the dissolution of our family. Only decades later would I understand that she didn't have the mental and emotional protection my dissociative state provided me. While I felt little emotion at all, Sandy was becoming increasingly unhappy. Though I couldn't see it at the time, my mother's lack of love and unkind treatment affected Sandy as much as it did me, though in different ways. Enough that Sandy would always suffer a distrust of other people which kept her from building strong open and straightforward relationships. Daddy and Grace married shortly after that in a small, informal wedding. Daddy moved into Grace's large, two story house. She had two boys of her own, and Sandy soon moved in with Daddy's new family.

Meanwhile, Mother met a man named Herman. If Mother seemed too stiff and emotionless for romantic relationships, she was also still a very pretty woman. Petite—only four feet, eleven inches and no more than a hundred pounds—she projected a deceptive sweetness and fragile neediness that would make men feel protective and important around her. I can remember Herman saying once of my mother, "She's little but oh, my!"

Mother encountered Herman through one of her few activities that still took her out of the house. My mother had always enjoyed square dancing, so much so that she had special square dancing outfits to wear for the dances. In fact, it was one of the few hobbies I knew of that my mother had enjoyed doing with my father during their college years and early married life. She'd stopped dancing as her obsessive-compulsive order worsened, insisting that as she was so short, germs might fall on her from her dance partners. By her divorce, she'd become a complete recluse. So my father expressed astonishment when she started dancing again with Herman.

As with my father, I felt no negative emotions about it. Herman seemed like a nice man. He treated Mother well and, by all appearances, made her happy. After a short courtship, they married. Now both my parents seemed happy. They'd both made good choices—for them, but not for me. Living with Mother and Herman, I felt like nothing more than an inanimate, lifeless household object. During dinner, our only time together, conversation wasn't exchanged. Mother and Herman usually had their noses in the newspaper.

My own routine was to finish my meal, push away from the table, and clean the dirty dishes in silence. Then I retreated to my bedroom. By this point I had both a television and a phone in my room, so that became my evening entertainment. After a year of living in a house of no warmth, feelings, or care, I asked Mother if I could move in with Daddy. After all, my sister was living there now. Why shouldn't I?

She shrugged. "Sure, it's up to you."

I called Daddy right away. "Daddy can I move in with you?"

"I'd love it, but I have to ask Grace."

After a couple days of anxious waiting, Daddy finally called. Grace was happy to have me, and her two boys were looking forward to my coming as well. I moved into Sandy's bedroom. She had twin beds, perfect for the two of us. Without Mother pitting us against each other, we chatted easily like best friends.

But Sandy was still around only at the dinner table and bedtime. She told me once that living with Mother had taught her staying intentionally out of the way was the only way to keep the peace. In contrast, my stepbrothers were at home most of the time. We spent hours in the den watching *I Love Lucy, American Bandstand,* and *The Ed Sullivan Show.*

At night, Daddy and Grace would go into the living room with a filled-to-the-brim alcoholic drink in their hands. Their voices grew animated, louder, as they refreshed their drinks. Sometimes, I could hear intense arguing. One evening, I overheard my stepmother saying, "Sue is dirty and stupid. She doesn't even know when to put her dirty clothes in the washer. And her hair looks like a bird's nest."

I felt hurt and lost, above all because I didn't know what I'd done wrong. I did the dishes every night. Never talked back. Put my clothes away. She'd only scolded me once for leaving my shoes downstairs. So why didn't she like me? I felt like trash, fit only for the dumpster. *Grace is right. I'm gross. She sees through the mess I am.*

One night Grace yelled at me for not making my bed, saying I was no good. I felt suddenly overwhelmed with a hate for myself and Grace. Feeling a sudden need for something, Someone, beyond myself, I raced into the living-room. Though Grace had never given any indication of faith in God, I'd once seen a Bible on a shelf among many other books. I didn't know much about the Bible, but I remembered leafing through its pages as a young child in Sunday school.

Grabbing the Bible off the shelf, I opened it up. My eyes landed immediately on a line of text that spoke directly to my heart: "God is our refuge and strength, a very present help in times of trouble."

CHAPTER EIGHTEEN

HELP

God is our refuge and strength, a very present help
in times of trouble.

—Psalm 46:1

The words I read were the beginning of chapter forty-six in a part of the Bible called Psalms. The words filled me with the sense of God's presence that I'd experienced that day with my friend Louise. Picking up the phone, I dialed her number with hurried fingers. "Louise, do you remember when you told me how God is our Father in heaven and that He loves and cares for me?"

She chuckled, "How could I forget that?"

"Well, you won't believe what happened. I just opened the Bible, and right there on the page were words from God telling me that He is our refuge and strength."

After I told Louise my story, she invited me to spend the night next weekend. But my improved spirits were dashed just a week later when I brought home my latest report card. Daddy looked over my very average grades with a frown.

"You have to change your priorities," he told me sternly. "You spend too much time with friends that aren't good enough for you. You should associate with such people as the daughters of my friends who are lawyers and judges. With proper influence, you can raise your standards, use the potential you have. Right now, you're like a singer with a gift of singing that never uses her voice."

At his words, my eyes grew wet. My head drooping, I berated myself. Daddy's disappointed in me and my friends. He thinks I could do better. But I can't! I'm stupid. I don't have much to offer. At least my friends accept me. Louise was elected cheerleader, and she still likes to be around me, so I can't be so bad!

At night when Daddy and Grace argued in angry voices that spoke of too much alcohol, I constantly overheard Grace putting me down and Daddy defending me. Close to a breaking point, I asked Mother if I could move back.

"Sure," she responded without a shred of emotion.

I hung up the phone, feeling dejected. Mother doesn't care one way or the other. I'm glad she didn't ask me why. I wouldn't want to tell her that Grace doesn't like me, thinks I'm stupid, ugly, and dirty. Besides, Mother might agree with her.

I moved back to Mother's house for a few months, caught between two unacceptable choices. Daddy loved me. Grace hated me. Mother didn't offer support or care. Nor did Herman. When I complained to Daddy on the phone, he called me back later the same day. "Grace is sorry she treated you so badly. She wants you to come back."

"Really Daddy?" Without hesitation and no resistance from Mother, I moved back. This time I kept out of Grace's way, turned the television louder, and didn't eavesdrop. Still, their quarreling reverberated through the walls, and Daddy started staying away for days at a time. Feeling guilt and shame for being the likely cause, I asked Daddy, "What can I do to make Grace like me?"

Daddy tugged at his shirt collar. "Why don't you clean the stove? It's caked with grime and grease."

My eyes narrowed. "Do you think she'll mind? Maybe she'll think I'm criticizing her housekeeping."

"You could be right. Why don't you ask her and see what she says?"

Grace denied my offer. My esteem took another nosedive. In the meantime, Daddy's drinking increased, and his ashtrays were filled with cigarette butts, his face no longer smiling, but stern. Over the next several years, I would find myself moving back and forth between my mother and father's house on a regular basis.

Still, despite inner torment, my high school years rolled on with support from Charlene, Louise, and Lyla. Though I had good times with my friends, I took no interest in academics. I often slept in my classrooms, couldn't concentrate on the teacher's lectures, and made no attempt to learn or achieve good grades. If I tried, I'd fail. So why try?

By this point, Sandy had left home to attend college at the University of California, Berkeley campus, in Berkeley, a suburb of San Francisco. In keeping with her green thumb, she was studying landscape architecture. Since this was a good eight-hour drive from San Diego, we saw her only on vacations.

During my senior year, I was once again called out of the classroom. I swallowed hard as I followed an office monitor down the hall, memories marching before my eyes. The nurse's office for a hearing test in elementary school. The principal's office for a change of schools in junior high. The counseling room for closed-door therapy. And now this.

The monitor led me to a small room next to the school office. A tall, slender woman with glasses offered me her hand, then motioned me to sit down. A folder rested on the table in front of her. "Sue, I've been looking forward to meeting you. How are you?"

"I'm fine." Looking at the folder, I forced a smile.

"You must wonder why you're here," she said as she picked up a folder. "Your teachers have requested you be administered a Stanford-Binet intelligence test." Her eyes searched my face. "Are you okay with that?"

Do I have any choice? I looked out the window. "Yes, sure."

"Good. Now I'm going to ask you some questions," she said with a calm, relaxing voice. "Don't rush. Take your time. Answer them the best you can. Are you comfortable? Are you ready?"

I dug my nails in my hands and took a deep breath. "Okay."

The questions varied from my sense of direction, mixing proportions, building stick houses, logic questions, vocabulary, understanding proverbs, and repeating numbers. After about an hour of testing, she stopped, looked over her papers, and grinned. "Sue, you did quite well. You are gifted."

Me? I left in shock, shaking my head to clear it. What will Mother think? She always thought I was stupid. Will she like me now, even ask me to move in with her and my step-dad again?

Rushing home, I quickly dialed her number. "Mother, I had a Stanford-Binet IQ test today. My score showed I'm gifted."

Mother sounded pleased. "I'll go to the library to get you some books on giftedness."

As soon as Daddy came home from work, I dashed over to him. "Daddy, guess what. I'm gifted, not stupid after all."

"Oh Suzie. I never thought you were stupid." He wrapped his arms around me. "That's great. Now that you're close to graduating from high school, you can go to college."

I looked down at my hands. "Daddy, I was planning on being a telephone operator. Now my sights are higher, knowing I can do college work. But my grades aren't good enough to be accepted in a college. I will need to go to a community college."

His lips tightened in a frown. "That's just a glorified high school."

I refused to let his disapproval discourage me. At last I had some hope for success. But what did it mean to be gifted? A lump formed in my throat as I read that gifted people display unusual abilities, are inquisitive, and have a variety of interests along with an abundance of energy. Those descriptions didn't fit me. I had no abilities or interests. My grades were average. My only need was to please others.

Still, it wasn't long before I'd graduated from high school and found myself on a bus headed to San Diego Community College. With new self-assurance, I made my way to my classes with folder and sharpened pencil, ready to take notes. I worked hard, listened hard, did all my homework, and was rewarded by receiving an A in all my classes.

By now I had noticed another girl sitting alone on the same bus each day. We disembarked together at the community college, but made no eye contact and walked in different directions to our classes. One day I mustered up my courage to sit next to her on the bus and introduce myself. We hit it off right away.

Diane proved to be a good conversationalist with a lighthearted personality and easy laugh. No surprise, since we rode the same bus to college, she lived only a few blocks from where I was living with Daddy. We soon became close friends. We hooped and hollered together at college parties, dancing ourselves silly to Little Richard, Buddy Holly, and Jerry Lee Lewis. We indulged in fast food together and chatted on the phone for hours.

Then on one eventful day, Diane and I were strolling toward my house when a black 1955 Chevy raced by. Suddenly, its brakes screeched. Then the car backed up to where Diane and I were walking. Two grinning young men with crew-tops were in the front seat.

One of the young men called out, "Hey Diane, haven't seen you since we graduated from high school. What's up?"

"Nothing much, just passing time. This is my good friend, Sue." Diane turned to me, indicating the two young men in the convertible. "And these two are Larry and Laurence, two of my best pals in high school."

"Hi, nice to meet you." Feeling shy, I avoided eye contact. Then the young man Diane had identified as Larry looked over at her. "Hey, we're on our way to go bowling. Why don't you join us?'"

"Can my friend come too?"

"Sure, jump in."

Diane and I climbed into the back seat. At the bowling alley, we had to use rented balls, and our scores reflected it. Laurence and Larry brought their own sixteen-pound balls and earned scores in the one-hundred-and-seventies.

"Wow!" I said. "You guys should enter a contest."

Larry grinned at me. "Actually, I did bowl in a junior national tournament a few years ago, though I only finished fourth." I learned he was being modest, since he was only in junior high when he won that distinction.

Besides being modest, Larry proved easy to talk to and a lot of fun. I found out that he was four months older than me, born August 22, 1941, and had been in the same high school class as Diane. Like me, he was studying at a college level, but he was also working in construction, driving heavy equipment.

Thoughts of Larry danced in my head after he and Laurence dropped Diane and me off. Would I see him again? Would he call me? I kept an ear out for the phone, and the instant it rang, I rushed over, grabbing the receiver from its cradle.

CHAPTER NINETEEN

DIVINE GUIDANCE

In their heart humans plan their course but God establishes their steps.

—Proverbs 16:9

My heart pounded when I discovered the caller was indeed Larry. From then on, we dated every weekend. He brought humor to my serious life, making me laugh by such antics as stubbing out cigarettes on his tongue. He would serenade me with his guitar, singing a popular song in my honor: "Oh, Suzie Q, I love you." We discussed everything from calorie-counting to politics, and he never made fun of my ignorance in certain school subjects. Sometimes when the mood struck us, we'd park his convertible on a curb, turn up the volume on the radio, and jitterbug to rock-and-roll music on the sidewalk. We fit together like two bodies in one soul.

One day the subject of Christianity came up. I'd known Larry and his family were from a Lutheran church heritage, which was fine with me, even though I had no real idea what I myself believed about

God at this point. When I made no response, Larry gave me a probing look. "You're a Christian, aren't you?"

I shook my head. "I believe in God. I believe in prayer. But I can't believe in Christ."

"Why not? Didn't you go to church as a child?"

"I went with my parents a few times when I was still in kindergarten," I explained. "But they weren't Christians. My mother is an atheist, my father agnostic. As for me, well, I remember the Sunday school teacher putting flannel graph pictures of Jesus with little children on a felt board. She said he loved little children. I felt that was stupid. How could he love me? He didn't know me. I think that was the last time I went to Sunday school."

Even as I was explaining this to Larry, an odd feeling squeezed at my stomach at the mention of Jesus. I'd forgotten until now how much I hated being made to sing songs about Jesus as a small child. Why did it bother me so? Why was I seeing the face of Jesus distorted in my mind?

I pushed my thoughts away. I could hardly tell Larry how I really felt. And I liked the idea of Larry being a Christian. There was something wholesome about a family going to church together. It gave me a feeling of safety. I know now that even then God was at work in my traumatized heart and mind.

Larry leaned forward. "Christ gave his life on the cross to save us from our sins because he loves us. And he didn't stay dead. He rose again, demonstrating his power over death and sin and guaranteeing we too can have eternal life."

Trying to please Larry, I nodded agreement as he spoke. Later he enrolled me in a confirmation class, where I learned about worship and basic Christian doctrine. I even went through baptism, but my doubts remained. I did believe in a God who'd given me the strength to endure horrific trauma. But why would someone's death and the shedding of his blood forgive sins? How could someone have that kind of power? Who was this Christ to make such claims?

Since my relationship with Larry was progressing rapidly, making me feel cared-about and secure for a change, I kept my doubts to myself. We'd been dating for over a year when Larry asked me one day, "Sue, are you free to go out to dinner with me Saturday evening? I have a surprise for you."

Christmas was just two weeks away, my nineteenth birthday two days after that. Was Larry planning on giving me an early Christmas or birthday present? When Saturday came, I went through my closet and picked out a brown taffeta dress with ruffles around the neck. I added a pearl necklace. After curling my eyelashes and applying makeup, I looked at myself in the mirror with approval. Larry certainly agreed by his expression when he picked me up.

"Wow, you look great!" he exclaimed, looking me up and down.

I put my hand on my heart in a faux movie star gesture. "Thanks!"

As Larry opened the front passenger door for me, I felt like a lady. His lady. The restaurant where he'd made reservations looked like a tropical paradise as we walked arm-in-arm across a small bridge that overlooked a pond alive with golden koi.

"Larry, isn't it beautiful?" I pointed out.

His finely-chiseled features were alight with a broad smile, his blue dress shirt the exact shade of his eyes, as he led me through the restaurant to a booth overlooking the bay outside. A warm glow of flickering candles illuminated our menus as we ordered a prime rib dinner with vanilla ice cream for dessert. After we finished eating, Larry took a little package wrapped in floral paper out of his pocket. My heart began racing as he offered me the present. When I opened it, I discovered inside an engagement ring with a sparkling diamond in the center.

Leaning forward, Larry placed his hand on top of mine. "Sue, will you marry me?"

"Yes! Yes!" I responded breathlessly. We walked out of the restaurant into a night sky brilliant with stars. I embraced them as a foreshadowing of a bright future ahead.

CHAPTER TWENTY

GOD'S LOVE

Consider the ravens: they do not sow or reap, they have no storeroom; yet God feeds them.

—Luke 12:24

Though not everyone was happy over our engagement. Larry's mother Cordy made it clear that she was upset. Larry was only nineteen years old, and his parents had just bought a new split-level house, assuming Larry would be sharing it with them for the next few years, at least until he graduated from college. Larry assured me that his mother would come to love me, but once again, I had to fight down a feeling of rejection and that I somehow deserved her obvious dislike of me.

Grace and Daddy, with whom I was living at the time, were in the living room reading the newspaper when I announced my good news. Daddy said immediately that he was happy for me and that he liked Larry's politeness and quiet manner. But Grace just rolled her eyes and told me I'd make a terrible wife. I didn't even know how to cook properly. I wasn't surprised at her reaction, since Grace had made clear she didn't like anything about me.

Larry and I were married on August 25th, 1961, just three days after Larry turned twenty years old. We drove to Victoria, Canada, for our honeymoon, staying at the Olde England Inn, where we slept in an actual canopy bed. Larry bought me my first cashmere sweater at the inn gift shop. Going back home to an apartment of our own made me feel complete at last.

Larry took his new responsibility as husband and provider very seriously. He no longer did silly stunts like putting cigarettes out on his tongue. We didn't dance on the sidewalks. If I acted too loud or silly in public, he'd tell me to act my age. This made me feel as though I had a halter around my neck reining me in. But Larry was right. I was now a married woman. Just five months after our marriage, I turned twenty as well, which meant neither of us were teenagers anymore.

For the first year or so of our marriage, Larry continued taking college courses while also working full time driving heavy equipment. I took a few courses at a community college as well, but I too was working fulltime by now at a telephone company two blocks from our apartment, where I'd landed a clerical position. Sitting at my desk and earning my own money made me feel important, that I was contributing to our marriage. When five o'clock arrived, I'd head home from my job, ecstatic with happiness that Larry and I were sharing the same closet space, eating in the same kitchen, sleeping in the same bed.

"What's for dinner?" Larry would ask.

"What do you want?" I'd respond.

"Anything that's easy."

That's the way Larry was, not demanding, always easy-going. Except in one area: church. Every Sunday without complaint, I would accompany Larry to church, where we would sit in the same pew with his parents and take communion together. The church sanctuary was beautiful with a glitter of red, blue, and yellow light shining through stained-glass windows. The preacher spoke of principles I believed in: honesty, love, respect, and loyalty.

But whenever I looked up at the large cross on the far wall above the sanctuary chancel, an agitation arose from deep within me. Being a master of disassociation by now, I would quickly turn my thoughts to the family breakfast of scrambled eggs, ham, and pancakes we always enjoyed with Larry's parents after church.

I loved married life and my new extended family. This consisted basically of Larry's parents. He actually had an older brother. But his brother had been fifteen when Larry was born, so Larry had grown up more like an only child. Especially once his brother married, as his brother's wife didn't get along with her in-laws. Reminiscent of my own family, Larry's brother and wife lived in the same town as we did, but neither of them showed any interest in being part of our lives, so we rarely saw them even on holidays.

Larry's parents were kind enough to me. Still, Cordy, my mother-in-law often reminded me that it was my fault Larry was a jack of all trades, but master of none because he'd married me instead of going to college. She made clear that by marrying me Larry had lost the opportunity to achieve all she felt he was capable of. This simply added another layer of pain for me to stuff away, but I kept my misgivings to myself and concentrated on my marriage, a loving relationship that bestowed on me a fresh gift of security every day.

Larry and I were blending as one. Television? He liked it. I didn't. Reading? I liked it. He didn't. Anger? He had a temper. I didn't. Moods? I was moody. He wasn't. Talkative? I was talkative. He wasn't. But we held hands as we worked out our problems, and after a year of marriage, my moods stopped, his anger lessened, and my spirit swelled with a growing passion for life.

Despite my agitation and distorted understanding of Jesus, my regular attendance and interest in serving others led me to become very active at the church we attended. I visited shut-ins, worked on fundraisers, and even became chairman of the Board of Human Care.

Pleased with my happy life and marriage at the young age of twenty, I drove one day to Mother's house to share my bubbling heart. Knocking on her door, I heard her call out, "Who is it?"

"Sue."

"Oh. Come on in." Mother's kettle was whistling when I entered the kitchen. "Would you like some tea?"

"Sure. Do have any cookies to go with it?"

"Help yourself to the pantry. See what you can find."

I found a package of Oreo cookies while Mother prepared two cups of tea. I joined her at the kitchen table and began to tell her of my good life as we sipped tea and nibbled at a cookie. Mother suddenly looked down at my feet and frowned. "Are you nervous? Why is your foot shaking?"

I hadn't even realized I was swinging a foot back and forth in excitement as I talked. I immediately locked my ankles. *I better appear calm. She might think I'm like Daddy, too excitable, mentally unstable!* "Mother, you know Larry and I have been married a year now. We have such a good marriage. I'm so happy."

She barely hesitated before saying flatly, "The only reason you're still married is because Larry is mature. You're sure not!"

I knew exactly what she was implying, and my shoulders immediately slumped as my self-esteem plummeted. *Don't feel good about yourself. You're worthless, nothing! All you're good for is to try to please others!* But I ignored the sudden knot in my stomach, commenting pleasantly instead on how good the tea was and her pretty new lace curtains.

"So what have you heard lately from Sandy?"

Mother was happy to shift the conversation from my doings to my sister, who had never returned to San Diego after graduating from Berkeley. "I'm glad Sandy lives so far away. I couldn't handle two of you living so close. I'd rather have you than her."

Mother had always praised Sandy as being smart and told me I was at best average. Now she was as critical of Sandy as of me. While it made me feel somewhat better not to be the only disappointment as a daughter, I felt sad at the way my mother put Sandy down.

By the time I could politely disentangle myself, I was glad to leave. As I drove away from my mother's house, I drew in a deep breath of fresh air and looked up at the blue sky overhead with its fluffy white clouds skittering across it. A slight breeze rustled through the trees as birds zipped from branch to branch. Once again, my dependable stabilizer, Nature, restored my mental balance.

So did going home to a husband who loved me and accepted me just as I was. Larry had an easy-to please attitude, whether it was the food I cooked, the clothes I wore, or how I expressed myself. He replenished my self-esteem, his love a soothing balm to the tormented soul I struggled so hard to keep locked deep down below the conscious surface of my mind.

Larry and I had been married two years when I found out I was pregnant. My heart leaped in joy, and I immediately called my father. "Daddy, guess what. I'm pregnant."

Daddy's voice on the phone sounded slurred, so he'd clearly been drinking recently. "So? Everyone has children."

His indifference was like a slap in the face. "But, Daddy, you're going to be a grandfather and I'm going to be a mother. Don't you care?"

He didn't reply.

The muscles in my face tightened. "I thought you'd be happy for me."

All I heard on the line was heavy breathing. "Daddy, are you okay?"

"I'm fine!" he answered sharply.

I swallowed back tears. Didn't Daddy care about me anymore? Was he going to have another breakdown? His words sounded so slurred. Was he drinking too much?

When I told Larry about the phone call, he shook his head in disbelief. "Your parents are sure different than mine. My parents were always there for me, supported everything I did. Still, I know your father loves you. He's probably just not feeling well."

Turning my gaze out the window, I intentionally tallied up my blessings. A caring, loving husband. A clerical job two blocks from home. Louise, my best friend, lived only a mile from our apartment. I wasn't as close to all my other friends as the passing years and our changing lives had separated us. Diane had moved to San Francisco. Lyla was busy working and dating, but we still saw each other as frequently as we could. Charlene and June as well. And now a new and wonderful blessing—a baby on the way.

Rushing to the library, I checked out and read Dr. Spock's book on baby and child care, which was then considered the supreme authority on the subject. I painted the nursery a light grey, combined with striped white-and-gray wall paper, white furniture, and bright yellow accessories. As my pregnancy progressed, my heart overflowed with joy.

Then on January 2, 1964, one of life's most precious miracles entered the world, Dena Louise Liston. When I placed my finger for the first time into her tiny hand and her precious little fingers wrapped around mine, it felt as though my bright future had indeed come to past. How could life get any better than this?

CHAPTER TWENTY-ONE

STRENGTH

Be strong in the Lord and His mighty power.
—Ephesians 6:10

Sadly, Dena's coos soon turned to angry cries. I had no breast milk to feed her, and her pink, little face would turn bright red as she screamed for sustenance. When I switched to a bottle, it constantly plugged up. But when I unplugged the nipple with a hot needle, the milk spilled out like Niagara Falls, choking her. Even once she was fed, her angry cries persisted.

To this point we'd been living in a rented apartment. Dena was two years old when we purchased our first home in El Cajon, a middle-class suburb of about 100,000 residents in a mountain valley about fifteen miles from San Diego. Her unhappiness followed her all the way into her school years. When she began kindergarten, she was shy, cried easily, and had few friends.

By this time Dena had a little sister, Donna, born on December 21, 1968. Donna was a sunny, smiling child who brought warmth and joy in our lives. Dena once drew a picture of Donna in her crib with the caption: "Happiness is having a little sister to play with."

In contrast, Dena's despondency grew to the point that she often cried when I took her shopping or we went out to dinner. She began shutting herself up in her bedroom. Worried, I would ask her, "Dena, what's wrong?" She just looked away. "Nothing." I wrung my hands until they turned red. What more could I do? I lavished both my daughters with hugs and kisses. Gave Dena plenty of attention and care. Home was a good, happy place. We took many family camping trips, hiked, played horseshoes, told silly made-up stories while roasting marshmallows over the campfire. But nothing seemed to make Dena happy.

During all these years, my mother's disinterest in me trickled down to my children. She didn't attend one birthday party, babysit, call them on the phone, take them out for a fun day, or even attend their graduations when the time came. I blamed myself, feeling that I didn't deserve more. Yet I kept up a good front. As always, I buried my feelings deep within the dark chambers of my mind. My mantra was to try harder. Be extra nice. Win one more friend. Earn a smile on someone's face. Be productive.

In contrast, my mother-in-law Cordy had by this point made a complete 180-degree changed in her attitude towards me. Over the years, she'd seen that I was both a good wife to her son and a good mother to her granddaughters. Instead of being critical, she'd become my greatest supporter. We spent a lot of time together, including being involved together in our church. In fact, when we moved and had to find a new church, she and my father-in-law actually changed churches to be with us, though it meant a long drive to Sunday services. Cordy was also a wonderful grandmother to my children.

One contributing factor might have been Larry's own success. He has over the decades remained a "jack of all trades" in that he has developed countless skills and job proficiencies. But far from accomplishing nothing because he married me, Larry had in time graduated from college *cum laude*, all the while holding good-paying construction jobs. He'd then become manager of an emulsion plant that produced materials for road construction. From there he'd climbed the ladder of corporate management to oversee several plants, and was honored by being mentioned in *Who's Who of America*, a publication listing notable men and women. My father had also been listed in the same book. I was so proud of them both.

While Larry climbed the ladder of success, I'd dedicated myself to our home and raising our children. But by the time I was thirty-two, both our children were in school, leaving me with an empty house during the school day, restless hands, and no abilities to cultivate. Providence stepped in when Charlene, a friend from junior high, called me. "Hey Sue. Why don't we teach swimming in the backyard school program?"

"Me?" I responded. "I can't swim that well."

"They'll teach you. Come on. It will be fun." Charlene convinced me to try. We went through the Red Cross swimming program, which improved my strokes and confidence. I ended up teaching my own class and eventually became the chairperson of the entire back-yard swim program in our area with some two hundred children.

One day Mother overheard me explaining with a voice of authority the requirements of a pool being acceptable for swimming lessons. She shook her head in wonder. "I thought you couldn't do anything!"

I ignored my mother's hurtful remark. Instead, I turned to my friends for affirmation. One day Linda, a good friend who lived across the street from me, invited me to go with her to a program called Bible Study Fellowship. BSF is an in-depth, interdenominational Bible study course with more than a thousand study groups in thirty-nine nations. I attended BSF with Linda for about a year, then stopped. By that time, I realized that despite all the years of rote attendance at church with Larry and his family, even teaching a children's Sunday school class, I didn't understand the Bible, didn't really believe in its teachings, nor did I enjoy the ladies in my class.

I was thirty-five when we moved from our first small house to a larger upper-class home in the same community of El Cajon. I could hardly contain my excitement as I decorated our new home with wallpaper and fresh paint, tiled the bathroom floors, and hung up fresh curtains. Neighbors stopped over to introduce themselves. They convinced me to join their tennis and golf club.

I also became active in the local Parent-Teacher Association (PTA), becoming hospitality and backyard swim chairwoman as well as organizing adult bridge and tennis teams for the parents. When the PTA awarded me the Honorary Service Award for outstanding work, I was close to collapsing in shock. For three years in a row, I was asked to consider allowing my name to stand for PTA president. Though flattered, I refused, deeming that post beyond my ambition or abilities. After all, I didn't consider myself a standout. I was just trying to stay afloat. Do the best I could. Please others. Work hard.

Still, I was excited enough at the honor of being asked that I once again called my mother. Maybe she would think more of me now. But when I told her my flattering news, she simply responded, "They must be desperate, digging at the bottom of the barrel."

Another stab to the heart. Still, she was my mother. Around that same time, Mother had suggested I go back to college, telling me bluntly, "You're going nowhere."

Despite a lump in my throat at her unkindness, I knew she was right. So at the age of thirty-eight, I enrolled in college. To my surprise, I enjoyed school. I took just two classes a semester, which left me ample time for my other activities.

By now Dena and Donna were growing up. By any objective standards, both seemed to be doing just fine. By high school, Dena had grown into a beauty with long, curly hair, large violet eyes, and a lovely smile. Boys were constantly calling her. She rarely disobeyed, did her chores without complaint, and maintained straight "A's" throughout junior high and high school.

Despite all this, just a few months before her high school graduation in 1982, Dena blurted out one night after dinner, "I feel like killing myself."

My body went rigid. "What?"

Dena fidgeted, drooped her head. "I feel like killing myself."

"Dena, how could you say that? You're so pretty and smart."

"You don't understand." Dena stomped out of the kitchen and into a world of crystal meth, marijuana, and hallucinogenic mushrooms, all easily obtainable in the 1980s. She would come home with her eyes dilated and red, fall onto her bed, and refuse to eat, turning a deaf ear to my pleas of concern.

Donna did well in school too. Outgoing, popular, with many friends, she finished elementary school with a medal for being the school's outstanding athlete. In junior high, she was named "best personality". In high school, she became a cheerleader as well as secretary of her class.

But by this time my worrying and concern for Dena had grown to the point I didn't know where to turn for help. Dena was finally arrested for drug use. Thankfully, I found a good lawyer who not only obtained her release, but was able to expunge her record. Dena stopped using drugs, but her inner turmoil continued.

Daddy came over occasionally during these years. I'd become deeply concerned about his mental stability, heavy drinking, and constant smoking. Daddy took Lithium, a common prescription for his manic-depressive disorder, but it didn't always help keep his moods on an even keel. I remember one painful memory when I accompanied him to the bank. He yelled at the tellers, insisting his money wasn't safe there, and drew out a large sum of money. I remember also stopping with him at businesses for which he served as their corporate lawyer. He would rant and rave at his clients, accusing them of not running their businesses correctly. I would feel like hiding my face in humiliation at his behavior.

But then, as when I was a child, his moods would abruptly switch. Our best times occurred over lunch, usually once a month, when laughter and easy conversation filled the air. In December, 1981, Daddy and I went out together to our favorite restaurant. He seemed unusually quiet and complained that people were staring at him. He also told me the combination of his Lithium prescription and alcohol consumption was causing his legs to shake.

Daddy died that same night. Years later I was told he'd committed suicide. I still wasn't a Christian at the time, but looking back, I realize he fought his battle alone because he did not know the hope that would eventually transform my own life. The hope and promise that God goes before us, fights for us, brings us peace, and redeems our souls into eternal life with Christ.

CHAPTER TWENTY-TWO

UNENDING TRIALS

The refining pot is for silver and the furnace for gold,
but the Lord tests the hearts.
—Isaiah 48:10

I 'd been taking college courses for a couple years when Larry
and I took off for the weekend with some of his work friends
to Lake Tahoe, a well-known ski resort. By this point, Dena
was twenty and in college studying computer science.
Donna was fifteen, so we had no concerns about leaving them at
home together for the weekend.

We had a wonderful day skiing in glistening-white snow, eating
in a fine restaurant, enjoying easy conversation and laughter with
our friends. In the evening, we all retreated to a large log cabin,
where we rehashed the day's best ski runs over hot chocolate. I was
just changing into my pajamas when our friend Jim yelled from
downstairs, "Sue, it's for you."

Who would be calling at ten p.m.? Running downstairs, I picked
up the phone. "Hello?"

"Hi, Mother." The voice on the phone was Dena's. "Are you having fun?"

"Yes. How are you?"

"F-Fine. I'm studying for my computer class. It's hard. I hope I don't fail."

"Oh, Dena, you always say that and then end up getting an A!" I reassured her.

"You're right. I'll let you go." I could hear Dena inhaling deeply on the other end of the line. "I just wanted to hear your voice."

I hung up the phone with a shake of my head. Why had Dena called? She sounded nervous. Probably over her computer exam. But then she was such a perfectionist.

We stayed two more nights, then flew home. When we arrived at eleven p.m., we found Donna sitting alone in the living room. She looked dreadful, her eyes red and puffy. Something was terribly wrong.

"I've been waiting for you to get home," she said. "I have some bad news. Dena's not here. She tried to commit suicide."

Feeling dizzy, I sat down on the nearest chair. "Where is she?"

"At the Alvarado Hospital's Mental Ward."

Larry just stood there, frozen, looking grief-struck. "Tell me what happened."

Donna's voice sounded muffled, unreal. "I thought I was coming down with a cold, so I stayed home from school today. Then I heard a noise coming from Dena's room."

Donna went on to describe how she'd found Dena sprawled out on her bed, her head hanging down over the edge. When Donna tried to awaken her, she'd remained limp and unconscious. That was when Donna found an empty vodka and pill bottle on Dena's bedside stand along with a suicide note. "I called the number on the pill bottle. The pharmacist who answered told me to take her to the hospital immediately, which I did."

"You saved your sister's life!" I assured Donna, wiping away tears.

"But how did you know how to drive?" Larry asked, "or find your way to hospital?"

Donna rolled her eyes. "I've driven more than you realize! And the hospital is just off the freeway. I've seen it many times. Besides, I had no choice. Anyway, they pumped Dena's stomach and said she'd be all right."

When I called the hospital, they told us Dena would have to stay several days for observation. The next morning, we went to visit Dena. She looked tired with puffy eyes, but was anxious to come home. Without wasting any time, we found a good psychiatrist and a counselor. Dena regained control of her life and from then on began to flourish. She took no more drugs, went on to complete a degree in computer science, found a good job, and eventually met the man of her dreams.

But if Dena's life now appeared worry-free, our younger daughter Donna was facing her own troubles. By her junior year of high school, Donna was a cheerleader, class secretary, and an excellent student. Then an undercover cop caught her throwing a wine cooler out of her car on the school parking lot. She was expelled and sent to an alternative school for problem teens. Her first week there, someone tried to sell her drugs in return for sex.

Meeting with her principal and guidance counselor, I convinced them that the alternative school would do Donna more harm than good. They agreed to let her come back to the regular high school. After graduation, she enrolled in Sonoma State College. One day, she called me. "Mother, my boyfriend just tried to strangle me. Oh no, he's here now!"

She hung up, leaving me frantic with helpless anxiety and fear. It was some time before I heard anything further, and what I learned left me furious and even more worried. Donna had been at a party when her boyfriend, who'd been drinking heavily, started an argument with her. They'd been outside alone in the yard when her boyfriend put his hands around her neck and began choking her. A neighbor had heard the commotion and called the police. By the time the police arrived, Donna had lost consciousness and was on the ground.

Even so, she refused to press charges. When I asked her why, she told me, "I love him! I want to marry him. Besides, he apologized, and I've accepted his apology."

But if she accepted it, I didn't! Especially when I found out this wasn't the first time he'd put his hands on her. After spending hours on the phone, Larry and I were able to get Donna into Cal State in Los Angeles, where she settled in well and began studying for a degree in special education. Life was finally running on the right track. I in turn continued my own college studies, working toward my goal to become a certified teacher.

But after eight years of part-time studies without missing a single class, I quit. The reason was my master teacher, the person under whom I was doing my practice teaching. I did everything I could to please her. I brought her cut flowers from my yard. I took pictures of her well-decorated classroom filled with kid's pictures and good test results. I maintained a good rapport with the children.

But nothing improved her low opinion of me. Her expression when she glared at me brought to mind my mother's and my sister's facial expressions when they were angry at me. When she yelled at the kids, stomped her feet, or swiped their desk papers onto the floor evoked my father's uncontrollable rages.

I kept my cool, but I was down to perhaps three hours of sleep at night, tossing, turning, worrying about what tomorrow might bring. In desperation, I tried acupuncture, herbs, hypnotism, visualization CDs, and various sleeping pills washed down with a glass of sherry. Knowing I was on a destructive course, I prayed every night for help.

God answered my call. My college supervisor witnessed how my master teacher treated me and transferred me to another school to finish my practice teaching. But by that point, I was so emotionally and physically spent that I resigned. Dark depression settled over me. I stayed in bed. When I did wake up, it was with a heavy head, reddened eyes, and blurred vision. Calling my mother, I told her I was depressed. Could I come over and see her?

She brushed me off, saying that I'd disturb her nap, then suggested coldly that I enroll in the Betty Ford Center, which was a treatment program for alcoholics. Not what I wanted or needed at all. My step-dad Herman told me to come over anyway. When I did, I found Mother outside, but when she saw me, she hurried into the house with her head down.

"Herman, why did she run from me?" I asked. "Why doesn't she ever come over to visit me? We only live twenty minutes apart."

He avoided my gaze. "She doesn't feel well."

Then Donna had an experience that pushed me down even further into my inner pit of darkness and depression. She was with a bunch of girlfriends in Tijuana, a city in Mexico that straddles the border with San Diego, when she stepped outside with a beer in her hand. Two police cars drove up.

One officer told her that drinking on the street was illegal and ordered her to get into his police car. She was taken away and assaulted.

When I heard the news, my soul, mind, and spirit reeled in misery. I also wanted the crime punished. I told Donna, "I'm calling the Tijuana police department to ask which policemen had that beat. I'm going to insist on a lineup. Then you can pick out your assailant."

Donna's face turned white. "I can't!"

"Okay, but you need at least to get a medical checkup and go to a professional counselor."

"I don't need a counselor," she insisted.

"Go just one time. If you don't want to go back, you don't need to."

Shoulders hunched, she finally nodded. A couple days later, we drove in strained silence toward a counselor I'd found in the yellow pages who specialized in trauma. As I gripped the wheel, memories of driving my father to a sanitarium hit me like a bolt. This was so similar, so unnerving.

We pulled up at an old Victorian house that looked more like a bed-and-breakfast than a trauma center. A woman with long, straight hair and kind blue eyes answered the door. "You must be Sue and Donna. I'm Lisa."

She motioned us to take a seat in the reception area, then engaged us in small talk about the weather, where we lived, and Donna's school before shifting the conversation to a serious note. "I understand your daughter has an issue you'd like me to help her work through."

When Donna made no response, twisting her long, blonde hair around her fingers, Lisa looked directly at her. "Let's step into my office where we can talk."

While she led Donna away, I stared out the window, where I could see life flowing along in its normal pattern. Mothers pushed baby carriages. Kids skipped over cracks. Elderly couple walked arm in arm. I was the one who felt completely out-of-step with life's normal pattern. The clock on the mantle slowly ticked the minutes away until Donna and Lisa reentered the reception area. Both were smiling.

"Donna is handling herself quite well," Lisa told me.

"Great!" I responded. "Thanks for your help."

Lisa put her arm around me. "How are *you* doing?"

I stiffened. "Fine!"

As we drove away, Donna told me firmly, "I'm not going to let that episode ruin my life. Did I tell you I went jet skiing yesterday with some good friends? I had a great time. My life isn't ruined. I'm going to be just fine."

And she was. From that point on, Donna bounced back like a ball. She continued her studies and became a special education P.E. teacher. While at Cal State, she also met a good-looking, hard-working young law student, whom she later married. Once he graduated from law school, they moved to San Diego, so Larry and I now had our youngest daughter and her husband living close by.

CHAPTER TWENTY-THREE

GOD'S INTERVENTION

For we know that in all things God works for the good of those who love Him, who have been called according to his purpose.

—Romans 8:28

Whether Donna felt she was fine, I knew I still had a job to do as her mother—to keep reassuring her she was still my precious little girl, no matter what trauma entered her life, and that I loved her. When her counselor called me a few days after our visit, I assumed it was a follow-up on Donna. To my surprise, Lisa asked, "Sue, would you consider counseling?"

I straightened up, startled. "I've never thought of it. I've never needed that kind of help." After a short pause, I added, "I must admit I'm depressed. Maybe you could help me."

"Well, why don't you come in, and we can talk about it?"

I did so. That decision at the age of forty-five began a journey into the hidden trauma of my mind. Our sessions took place in a small room furnished with a couch, two chairs, and three end tables.

I still saw no real need for a counselor. But Lisa asked with genuine warmth and interest about my week, my family, and what I enjoyed doing. To have such an attentive and encouraging listener was in itself a comfort, and before long we'd established a close bond. I trusted Lisa. She didn't pass judgement on me, didn't minimize my depression, or give me empty encouragement. Instead, she allowed me to feel my pain and work through it. During our weekly sessions, I felt relaxed as though I finally had permission to truly be myself.

But when Lisa asked about my childhood, I brushed it off. "Oh, it was nothing really out of the ordinary."

"How so?"

Shrugging my shoulders, I told Lisa about my Daddy's mental breakdowns, Mother's lack of interest in me, strangers living in my home, the renter who'd put my hand down his pants and the nudist who'd exposed himself to me.

Lisa's eyebrows rose high. "Sue, you are in denial. Your childhood was very dysfunctional."

She leaned forward. "When you think of your childhood, how did you feel about yourself?"

I shifted in my seat, my heart pounding unreasonably and a strange feeling of shame rising up in me. "I always felt stupid and ugly. I constantly asked myself why I said that, did that, acted like that. But that was okay. My needs weren't important. My goal was always to please others, so I learned to just ignore my dark places, keep busy, and work on gaining acceptance and respect."

"Sounds like you're a strong person," Lisa commented.

I looked at her directly. "Yes. Ignoring pain and discomfort is the answer."

Gradually in the safety net of Lisa's office, I allowed my buried pit of despair to surface, be looked at, and understood. Only then did I realize how deeply my dysfunctional life had affected my tormented psyche. But after seeing Lisa for months, I was still popping pills and drinking alcohol to sleep. Lisa told me bluntly, "You need to stop your self-destructive habits, or I can't see you anymore."

I did stop. As I came to realize my childhood family was dysfunctional, not me, my need for sleeping aids gradually diminished. After a year of counseling, Lisa encouraged me to return to my teaching program, even writing a letter of recommendation to the school board. Within another year, I graduated and began substitute teaching two days a week.

My life now appeared perfect. I had a respectable job, good friends, an adoring husband, children making a good life for themselves. My sister wasn't so fortunate. She'd met her future husband at Berkeley University. They both graduated, she in landscape architecture, he in architecture. She helped her husband find city approval with her landscaping designs along with his architectural designs. But since they both stemmed from dysfunctional families, their marriage foundered. Like my father, Sandy found solace in heavy drinking. After twenty-three years of disunion, my sister and her husband divorced.

Thankfully, at this point Sandy stopped drinking. She also moved back to San Diego. After Mother's comments to me, I doubt she shared my excitement in her move. But our relationship soon followed a similar pattern as in our childhood. Sometimes Sandy was glad to see me, while at other times an undercurrent of animosity and jealousy surfaced with her biting comments and a controlled brooding rancor against me.

I just let it go, trying to keep any friction out of the sisterly relationship we had most of the time. My life was good. I tried my best to keep it that way. So why did I still feel that undefinable emotional pain in my chest? What more could I want?

What does it mean? I asked myself desperately. *I have everything I want. Don't I?* I was still counseling with Lisa, but my therapy had basically come to a standstill. I needed to look elsewhere if I was to find an answer. But where?

Then one day, like an angel coming down from heaven, Nancy, a friend with whom I'd shared tennis games and heart-to-heart conversations over the past ten years, invited me to go biking with her at Lake Murray. The lake was actually a man-made reservoir near San Diego and a popular recreation site. Nancy was standing by her car when I drove up. The day was beautiful with clouds drifting through a tranquil sky, cormorants perched on rocks, and flocks of ducks floating in clear water. But as we lifted down our bikes, I found myself blurting out, "Nancy, I feel miserable."

"Why?" Nancy asked. "What's going on?"

"My counselor has helped me understand myself better. But I've been left with a growing pain of indescribable sadness. I don't know what it means."

Nancy took my hand. "Let's pray. God, help Sue to find her way with peace and understanding."

Her suggestion wasn't a surprise to me since over our years of conversation, I'd learned that Nancy had a deep personal faith. Her prayer restored a measure of calmness to my heart. When she finished, she looked up at me. "Sue, I feel God has already answered my prayer. I just received the new Grossmont College catalogue.

There's an inner childhood workshop being offered. I believe God is telling you to sign up for it."

My eyebrows knit together in a frown. "I don't want to work with my so-called inner child. I'm not a child any more. That sounds infantile and silly!"

But rejecting her suggestion made me feel even more miserable. In the following weeks, a darkness filled my soul that I couldn't shake off. My spirit felt twisted, inside out. Though Larry insisted I attend the Lutheran church with him every week, I'd long pushed away any real belief in church teachings. Still, I could not deny the sense that this was not just normal emotions of depression, but an actual spiritual battle playing out in my mind. It was as though God was pulling me forward, but the devil was pulling me backwards.

In desperation, I finally signed up for the inner child workshop. The teacher was a tall woman with short, curly hair named Dr. Miller. Introducing herself as a psychologist, she explained that by unlocking our painful past and unfulfilled childhood needs, we would connect and nourish the relationship between ourselves and others. She proceeded to show movies of kids laughing, playing on swings, monkey bars, and jungle gyms.

As I watched, disturbing emotions flooded my soul. My stomach tightened. My hands turned clammy. I shut my eyes in denial, pushing my feelings away. Once I regained my composure, questions swarmed in my head. Why were these images evoking such strong emotional pain? My memories of elementary school were happy ones. I'd had friends. I'd enjoyed playing on the school playground and participating in games. I'd been an athletic child, excelling in sports and always cheerful.

At least that was how I remembered my childhood. For our next class, Dr. Miller asked us to bring in a stuffed animal. I didn't bring one. I'd never had a stuffed animal since moving from my first home in La Mesa, and I didn't want one now. The others arrived with their stuffed animals held tightly to their chest. I found that very unappealing—grownups acting, wanting to be like children.

Next, Dr. Millar wanted us to bring in a baby picture. I didn't even possess a baby picture. Mother had thrown them all away except for a single picture taken when I was a toddler. Locating it, I brought the picture to class. With a smile, Dr. Miller told us to pass our pictures around the class. At her instruction, my heart began pounding hard, its pulse throbbing at my temple. Sweat beaded on my brow. A wave shame and hate swept over me for what the picture represented—a stupid, ugly little girl. Instead of passing my picture around, I covered my face and sobbed.

When the class was over Dr. Miller took me aside. "Sue, you seem deeply disturbed. I give counseling sessions as well as group therapy. May I suggest we meet individually for a while? Then when you're ready, you can join my support group."

The episode with the picture had shocked me, making me realize I did indeed have deep-seated emotional pain. For the next few months, I attended individual counseling with Dr. Miller, until she felt I was ready to join her support group. The group met in Dr. Miller's home. When I walked into the living-room, I noted that most of them were close to my own age. They looked relaxed and normal enough in casual jeans and T-shirts.

Sitting in a circle, each member spoke about their abusers, often members of their own family, and the resultant pain from being physically abused and molested. Some told of making up imaginary friends and talking to them in the quiet of their bedroom. I felt sorry for the others. After all, I'd always had friends. I hadn't been abused physically or molested by family members. Sure, a stranger had molested me, but that wasn't a big deal. I'd survived it.

Maybe I am not as bad off as I thought, I told myself.

Co-dependency was also discussed. This included feeling overly responsible for other people's emotions and actions, a need to control events, having problems making decisions, feeling trapped in relationships, and finding trouble in completing projects. None of these fit me. My life was healthy and happy. So why did I still have that nagging, indefinable pain? Why did the movies of kids playing on the playground bring such distress? Why did I cry when asked to pass around my childhood picture?

I continued attending the group therapy. Dr. Miller focused on helping us give ourselves affirmations—that we were precious, wonderful, worthy of goodness, that we were not alone. We learned to share our source of inner pain, write and draw our inner feelings, understand the consequences of dysfunctional behavior. But none of this assuaged my inner pain. Then one day Dr. Miller introduced a new exercise.

"Now, I'm going to lower the lights and put a chair in front of you," she told us. "You are to visualize your offender sitting in front of you. Hurl your past anger, hate, and bitterness on the abuser. Then forgive. Be healed."

I wasn't worried, just curious. After all, I had never cast blame on anybody. Who would I see? My mother, maybe? Father? Sister? Or perhaps some stranger who lived in my house?

When it was my turn, I calmly took a seat, folded my hands on my lap, and looked at the empty chair placed in front of me. Dr. Miller dimmed the lights. "Okay, Sue, I want you to visualize your abuser and release your feelings."

I was stunned to feel myself growing rigid in fear. I gasped out, "It . . . it's my mother! Her face looks like the devil, red faced and hateful. Oh, no! She's shooting out red laser beams from her eyes. They're piercing my soul." Wrapping my arms around my body, I rocked back and forth. "Bats are coming out of my pores!"

Dr. Miller placed her hand gently on my shoulder. "Just let the bats leave through your orifices—ears, nose, and eyes."

My muscles tightened even further. "They won't leave. They're surrounding me."

Suddenly, Dr. Miller shrieked, "I see demons around you, inside you."

With my hand covering my mouth in horror, I hysterically lunged toward her door, threw it open, then slammed it shut behind me. Racing to my car, I drove home as fast as I could. *What's going on? Why did I see my mother like that? Her face was pale, showed no expression, anger or otherwise. And why the bats? Where did they come from? I've never given bats any thought. I'm not even afraid of them!*

Desperate for solace and understanding, I called my friend Nancy. Though we didn't attend the same church, I knew from past conversations that she believed in the same biblical teachings about evil and satanic powers I'd heard over the years attending church with Larry. When I told her of how I'd seen a demonic apparition of my mother, she gasped. "What are you going to do?"

"I have to see Dr. Miller again," I responded.

"I know you're a normal person, sane in every way," Nancy reassured me firmly. "Go back to her. See what she says you should do."

With shaking fingers and a faint heart, I called Dr. Miller. She sounded taken back when she realized who was calling. After a long pause, she said, "I didn't know if I'd hear from you again."

"Are you willing to see me?" I asked urgently. "I am in desperate need of help. How could I see my mother that way? Do you really think there were demons around me? What am I supposed to do?"

As she paused again, my heart fell. Then she said, "We'd better not meet in my home anymore. When you left, I saw demons that looked like green globs in my house. I had to scoot them out with a broom." Then she blurted out, "I tried to burn your files. They resisted catching fire, but finally burnt. Let's meet in my vacation cabin up in the Cuyamaca Mountains."

After waiting several days, I set my jaw in determination and drove up into the mountains to the address she'd given me. When I arrived at her wooden cabin, Dr. Miller was outside on her porch, sweeping. I yelled out my car window. "Hi."

She looked startled, her smile forced. "You can park in the driveway. I'll meet you in the back of the house on the deck."

When I made my way around to the back deck, I found a cushioned chair and plopped down, holding my head in my hands. Dr. Miller came up to me with a small bottle in her hand.

I raised my head. "Why are you carrying that bottle? What's it for?"

"It's holy water, used for protection against any demonic encounter." Unabashedly, Dr. Miller opened the bottle and sprinkled water around me.

I felt weird, knowing she felt she had to protect herself from evil spirits lying within me. Dr. Miller then brought forward another chair to sit in, but left a full ten feet between us. She paused, looking bug-eyed, then told me bluntly, "I don't think I can help you. What you need is spiritual deliverance. Would you consider going to my Episcopal Church? I'm sure my priest there, Father Allen McNeil, could help you."

My eyes blurred with tears. As I left, my feet felt like they belonged to someone else. But I couldn't deny the truth in Dr. Miller's words. I needed spiritual help!

CHAPTER TWENTY-FOUR

EVIL THWARTED

I give them eternal life, and they shall never perish,
no one will snatch them out of my hand.
—John 10:28

Grimly determined now to pursue a solution, I called Dr. Miller's church the very next day. Within a few days, I found myself driving into the church parking lot. On this weekday, the parking lot was nearly empty. Taking a deep breath, I marched toward the church with my head held high. *I need to be here, do this. I need to be here, do this.*

My confidence fell once I walked into the imposing church reception area. Would the demonic forces Dr. Miller insisted were inside me show themselves? Or was I just crazy and would be declared insane? I forced myself to walk forwards toward the matronly older woman in a flowered dress behind the church's reception counter. "Hi. I'm Sue. I have an appointment to see the pastor."

She smiled. "Oh yes! Have a seat. The pastor will be here shortly."

I slumped into a chair set against the wall and closed my eyes.

"Are you okay?" the receptionist called out.

I nodded without opening my eyes. "Yes, I'm just resting."

I didn't open my eyes until the receptionist announced the pastor's arrival. Father Allen proved to be a middle-aged, rotund man with thinning red hair and bushy eyebrows. He gave me a hearty handshake. "So nice to meet you, Sue. Please follow me down the hall into my office."

The hall was narrow and dimly lit. Swallowing down fear, I forced my limp legs to follow Father Allen. He waved me into an office decorated with pictures of Jesus, a statue of hands folded in prayer, and a plaque stating: "Jesus loves you. Peace be with you."

I felt uncomfortable as I sank down into the seat he indicated. Father Allen sat down in a swivel chair behind his desk. His eyes as he swiveled to face me held kindness and compassion. But I avoided his gaze, digging my fingernails into my palms.

He leaned forward, "So what brings you here, Sue?"

I felt my body shrink back. "Dr. Miller, who attends your church, is also my counselor. She sent me here. She thinks I'm demon-possessed."

His bushy eyebrows raised. "So what do you think? What is your religious background?"

I breathed rapidly in and out before I could answer. "Well, I attend a Lutheran church every Sunday with my husband. I am a Steven's Minister there, am chairman for Human Care, and I visit the homebound."

Father Allen's gaze grew probing. He rubbed the back of his neck. "Then I assume you've accepted Jesus as your Savior?"

I looked down at the floor. "No, I haven't. In fact, I can't."

"Why do you say that?" he asked.

"I don't like talking about Jesus, saying His name, or even thinking about Him. I don't like looking at crosses either. I never have. I've tried to stop thinking that way, but I can't."

I suddenly couldn't go on. I found myself struggling to breathe, then began to choke. Father Allen looked concerned. "Would you like some water?"

"Yes, please."

Father Allen immediately rose from behind his desk and left the office. He came back with a glass of water, which he handed to me, then gently patted my back. "I sense you have several demonic spirits oppressing you. Would you be willing for a prayer team to work with you?"

I took a few gulps of water, but it didn't settle the uneasy stirring I felt in the pit of my stomach. "Yes, if you think it would help. I'm willing to do anything that might heal my troubled spirit."

Father Allen scheduled a meeting with the prayer team. When I drove back up to the church for the scheduled meeting, I had to fight my desire to turn around and drive home. *What am I doing here? What's going to happen to me?*

But I knew I had to do this. I couldn't keep running from myself. My legs felt like rubber as I walked across the parking lot and entered the church. Father Allen met me. "Great seeing you, Sue. Now just follow me into our chapel, where I'll introduce you to the prayer team."

I followed him into a small chapel with stained-glass windows. At the front was an altar where candles burned. Above the altar hung a good-sized cross. On the walls were pictures of apostles, angels, Mary, and baby Jesus. As we entered, Father Allen indicated two women sitting in a pew. "I'd like to introduce you to Cleo and Joan. They'll be working with you."

Cleo was about my mother's age with a short salt-and-pepper perm and a steady, penetrating gaze behind a pair of glasses. Joan was much younger, perhaps thirty years old, with long, wavy hair and a round face. She looked apprehensive. *Is she afraid of me?* I wondered as we greeted each other with thin smiles.

I slid into a pew behind the two ladies. Scooting in next to me, Father Allen asked, "How are you feeling?"

I wrung my hands. "I'm fine, but don't bring up sin, sex, or Jesus." *Where'd that come from? I'm usually not that bold.*

Father Allen rested his hand on my shoulder. "We won't encourage or force any subject that you wouldn't agree to. But the more we know you, the better we can help you. Is there anything you would like to talk about? Or problems you've been wrestling with?"

My posture slumped as I brought up my negative self-talk and self-hate, visions of burning crosses, coffins, men in black cloaks, and the cackling of witches.

Cleo looked over her glasses. "Have you been to a counselor?"

"I've been to several, including Dr. Miller, one of your parishioners. She is the one who sent me here. She said she felt I was demon-possessed."

The two women didn't flinch at the thought, their gaze calm and compassionate. Had they worked with people like me before? Was that why they'd been asked to be part of a prayer team? Father Allen looked at me directly. "Do you mind if we lay hands on you and pray over you?"

"No," I responded. But I clamped my eyes shut, and I could feel perspiration forming on my brow.

Father Allen and the two women laid their hands on my shoulders and began speaking in a babble I couldn't interpret. I had enough church experience to know this was called speaking in tongues, one of the gifts of the Holy Spirit according to the Bible. But as soon as they started speaking, something inside me shifted into a dark, wild side like a Dr. Jekyll turning into Mr. Hyde. My face twisted. My fingers curled like claws. Growling noises came out of my mouth. I hissed and fell out of the pew. Landing on the floor, I began rolling around, still growling. Not just my forehead, but my entire body was now drenched with perspiration.

Father Allen took a small cross off the wall. Kneeling down, he held the cross in front of me and yelled, "Leave Sue in the name of Jesus."

I found myself returning to normal, but now I felt deep shame and disgust for my deranged behavior. Jumping up, I dashed out of the chapel and raced toward my car, much as I'd done at Dr. Miller's house. Fearful someone would see my sweat-drenched hair and clothes, I flung my car door open and fell into the front seat. *What just happened? Where did that come from? Am I still me?*

Pulling down the rearview mirror, I examined my face. It looked no different than usual except for my stringy hair and smeared mascara. Regaining my composure, I drove home, where normalcy waited for me. Dark clouds loomed overhead, and as I drove, I heard a rumbling in the distance. Was that thunder? Sure enough, rain began to pelt my car. As my windshield wipers oscillated back and forth, my mind traced their rhythmic motion.

Just what I needed! A storm to match my mixed-up brain! What will Larry's reaction be when he sees me and hears my story? Will he be afraid of me? Will he start watching me like I did my father, not knowing when I might lose control and turn into a crazed person?

I shoved my emotions down into a safe place, employing techniques of rationality and positive thinking I'd learned over the past years of counseling. Gradually, my jaw loosened, my taut neck muscles relaxed, and the pounding rain became a welcome backdrop to my settling mind. *Stop worrying, Sue! You've been married to Larry over thirty years. You've built a respectable life together. Larry may be as shocked and confused as you are, but he knows you're not crazy!*

By now I was turning into my gated driveway. Parking my car next to Larry's, I headed inside. Larry was in the living-room, watching the news. My words burst out. "Larry, I just had the worst experience! Something exploded out of me, changed me into a demonic creature!"

Larry's mouth fell open. "What?"

Jumping up from his easy chair, he rushed over and wrapped his arms around me. "Sue, you're trembling! Here, sit down. Now tell me what happened."

Melting into his arms, I let Larry settle me onto the couch. After I told him my experience, he pulled me close. "Sue, I know you. You've done nothing wrong. If there really is any demonic influence, I blame your parents. Who knows what happened to you all those years with renters living there and no protection or security from you parents."

I gave a shudder. "But my behavior was so exaggerated, hostile, and aggressive, not like me at all. How could my parents cause that kind of behavior?"

Larry's eyes looked deeply into mine. "Sue, your mother gave you no love or care. Your father, who did give you support and encouragement, had to be institutionalized for years at a time due to his mental illness. Strange men lived in your house and molested you. The truth is, I don't know how you turned out so well. You are a great mother, wife, and person."

I let out a sigh of relief. "Thanks for being so understanding. You are truly a gift from God. But I wish my aversion to crosses and Jesus would leave. When I picture Jesus, He turns into a ghoul with bovine teeth, wrinkled skin and bulging eyes of hatred. I bet you didn't realize that, did you?"

Larry looked surprised. "No, I sure didn't! Why did you never tell me? How have you managed all these years to go to church, serve on committees, even teach Sunday school, if that's the way you've been feeling?"

"I ignore those images," I explained. "Just as I ignore any other bad feelings and memories. It's as though they aren't really connected to me. I try to do what's right and be helpful. As to telling you, that would just make my inner problems and images more real and cause more upset to both of us."

Larry nodded. "I understand, but I'm glad you told me now. It changes nothing between us."

I leaned into him, my anchor and support, but I couldn't completely banished the unsettling memories of the afternoon. How could I have been holding inside such bizarre behavior? Why would my voice change into angry growling and hissing? What could possibly have prompted me to throw myself on the floor and roll over and over like a dog?

"Larry, do you think I should go back to that church for help?" I asked. "I've kept a tight lid all these years on the horrors locked away in my mind. Do I even want to open it up and let all that horridness out?"

Larry looked thoughtful. "If you think you can handle it. It does sound to me from your description of what happened that there may be demonic forces torturing your mind. If so, then you do need deliverance and healing. Maybe we need to attend the Bible study at church and see if we can find out what the Bible says about demonic possession and God's protection against Satan."

I looked down at my knotted fists. "I tried studying the Bible, but it was too hard to understand."

Larry jumped up from his seat. "I read something in the Bible that speaks specifically to our spiritual battle with the evil one and how to defeat Satan."

Coming back with a Bible, Larry sat down again beside me and rustled through its pages until he found what he was looking for. Glancing at the open page as he began to read, I could see that it was the sixth chapter of the epistle to the Ephesians:

> Finally, be strong in the Lord and in his mighty power. Put on the full armor of God, so that you can take your stand against the devil's schemes. For our struggle is not against flesh and blood, but against the rulers, against the authorities, against the powers of this dark world and against the spiritual forces of evil in the heavenly realms. Therefore put on the full armor of God, so that when the day of evil comes, you may be able to stand your ground . . . In addition to all this, take up the shield of faith, with which you can extinguish all the flaming arrows of the evil one
>
> —Ephesians 6:10-16

CHAPTER TWENTY-FIVE

OUR ENEMY

For we wrestle not against flesh and blood, but
against . . . the spiritual forces of evil in the heavenly
realms.

—Ephesians 6:12

Maybe I'd heard these verses sometime over the years of attending church. But now they made sense as never before. Forces of evil that were not flesh and blood, but spiritual—surely that was what I'd experienced. By the time Larry finished reading the passage, my breath was coming in short gasps.

"Is there someplace in the Bible that speaks of the devil like a roaring lion?" I asked. "That's how it feels. I growl, and my fingers turn into claws, ready to tear me apart."

"Those words sound familiar. Why don't we look it up." Larry got up again. He returned shortly with a Bible concordance. "Okay, I found it in 1 Peter 5:8: 'Be alert and of sober mind. Your enemy, the devil, prowls around like a roaring lion looking for someone to devour.'"

My thoughts were galloping like a bloodhound. Sure, I'd lived through a difficult childhood. But God had rescued me. Brought me to the right people at the right time. Given me the ability to make healthy decisions. Helped my children to rise above their battles. Given me an adoring Christian husband. So this other demented side of me was a total shock. How had this happened?

Closing the Bible, Larry looked at me with concern, "Are you okay? Are you planning to go back to that church?"

"Yes, I think so. If they can help me get to the bottom of this, it is worth pursuing."

"Well, with your determination you can do it." Larry returned to reading his newspaper. I headed to the kitchen to begin preparing supper. I found his easy dismissal of my narrative actually comforting. *Larry doesn't seem worried about me. so I'm not worried about me either!*

But as I climbed into bed that night, I could feel a tightness in my chest. *What's going to happen when I go back to that church? Am I going to lose my mind? Become crazed like my father?*

I awoke to bright sunshine. Yesterday's storm was over. So was the storm in my mind. *I'll be okay. I always am.* I called the church and made another appointment with Father Allen. When I arrived, I found the same trio of Joan, Cleo, and Father Allen waiting for me. Father Allen gave me a vigorous handshake. "Hi Sue, I'm so glad you came back."

"Yes, when you ran away last week, we were concerned you wouldn't come back," Cleo said with a smile. "I'm so glad you did. We're anxious to help you—with God's help of course."

"We're honored to do so," Joan added, laying her hand on her heart.

"The way I look at it, I don't have a choice," I responded. "How can I live with something so abhorrent, so different than me? I want it gone, out of me."

I added hopefully, "Or maybe it's not there anymore."

Father Allen put his hand on my shoulder. "Let's go into the chapel and get started."

With sudden reluctance, I followed the others into the chapel. As I took a seat, Joan and Cleo scooted into the pew beside me. Once again, my insides rumbled in agitation as I took in the large, wooden cross behind the altar and the picture of Jesus on the wall facing me. A cold shiver ran down my spine. *Why do I feel such a revulsion against Jesus and the cross?*

Father Allen remained standing as he addressed me. "Sue, I think we should have a holy sacrament at our meeting today by serving the Eucharist. Jesus commanded the disciples to eat bread and wine in memory of Him."

I shrugged, "That's okay with me. My Lutheran church celebrates the Eucharist every Sunday."

In a few minutes, Father Allen came back with a tray that held a platter of wafers and a bronze goblet. The moment he raised it in front of my face, it was as though a different person rose up inside of me. A very angry person whom I didn't even know. My voice became harsh, deep, and gravelly. Balling my hand into a fist, I swung at the tray, knocking it out of Father Allen's hands. The wafers flew, and the wine splattered. As though a violent stranger, this other person inside of me slapped my head over and over again.

Father Allen shouted, "In the name of Jesus, flee from Sue."

The other person inside me put its hands over my ears. "I'm not listening! You can't make me do anything I don't want to do. I'm here to stay!"

Joan and Cleo were now standing over me, one on each side. Placing a hand on my shoulder, they began praying in tongues. Now another person seemed to rise up inside me. It bared its teeth and cackled, "Try, try, try, you fools! You're powerless against me."

At that moment, my neck jerked sharply back over and over again. My teeth ground together in such violence that I chipped a tooth. I fell to the floor, tossing and turning. Sweat poured out of my body.

Then, just as before, I abruptly switched back to my normal self. Once I regained my composure, I told my companions apologetically, "I'm so sorry and ashamed. I have no idea why I acted this way. There's no doubt I need your help. Can I come next week?"

"You're a brave lady," they assured me. "Please do come back. God will bring healing."

With my head hanging low, my hair wet and stringy, and my clothes sticking to me from perspiration, I once again dashed from the church to my car. Thorny, confused emotions filled my mind. How could I act out such revolting behavior? I'd always tried to be well-mannered and polite. I would never of my own accord act like an animal, growl and hiss, cackle like a witch, or fall to the floor, twisting and turning. Were satanic forces trying to destroy me? Was I trying to destroy myself? And how was it that I could just switch back to being me in a split second? It was as though something was turning me off and on like a faucet.

As I drove, I began to pray. That might not make sense, considering my reaction inside the church. But if the thought of Jesus or a cross evoked such bizarre images in my mind, since childhood I'd still recognized a higher Power in this world, a Peacemaker, if I didn't quite know who he was, who heard and answered prayer. "Please help me overcome this evil force that lives within me."

The plea brought some sense of peace. But as I turned into my driveway, the reality of what had happened at the church slapped me in the face. *What do I look like? Will my distorted insides show through? Will Larry notice my chipped tooth?*

"Larry!" I yelled as I ran into the house. He was nowhere in sight. Opening the door onto our back deck, I called, "Larry, are you outside?"

"I'm out here planting some tomatoes," I heard him call. As I emerged into the back yard, he stepped into view. "How'd it go at the church?"

"Unreal, like it happened to someone else." As I sank down onto a patio chair, Larry walked over to join me. His eyebrows rose as he took in my sweaty hair and clothing. "It looks like you had a hard time."

My voice felt as though it was emerging from a long, dark tunnel. "No, I'm fine. But I must admit I was pretty shocked at what happened. You know I take Eucharist at our Lutheran church every Sunday. But today, I switched into another state of mind and pushed the communion elements off the tray. Then I fell to the floor, twisting and turning, just as I told you last time."

"Wow, that does sound bizarre." Larry leaned forward to look at me more closely. "Sue, did you chip your tooth?"

"You noticed! Yes, I did, though I'm not sure exactly how. But don't worry, I'm okay."

"That doesn't sound okay! I don't think you should go back," Larry said in a determined voice.

I ran my fingers through my stringy, wet hair. "I have to. How can I live with something so monstrous inside me? Do you have any other suggestion for delivering me from such evil?"

Larry took my hands in his. "I suppose you're right. But I hate the thought of you chipping your teeth or hurting yourself in any other way."

"I'm fine." I glanced at my watch. "Oh, I'd better hurry. I have a bridge party to get ready for."

Larry shook his head in disbelief. "You're going to a party after what just happened to you"

I shrugged. "It's like it happened to someone else. Not me at all."

I couldn't go to a party with sweat-drenched hair and clothing, so I headed to the bathroom. I was stepping into the shower when I noticed the black and blue bruises all over my legs. What had I done to myself?

I'll be okay, I reassured myself as I showered. *I'll wear long pants. And hopefully no one will notice my chipped tooth.*

As I dressed, I glanced in the mirror. I looked tired with dark shadows under my eyes, deepened facial lines, and my complexion pale. *Makeup should do the trick.* Once I'd applied liquid facial makeup, blush for my high cheekbones, and thick mascara, I looked okay. Maybe even better than okay.

The bridge party was at the home of a friend named Becky, about a thirty-minute drive. Parking outside, I gave my face a final check in the rearview mirror. *Are my eyes red? Do they show fear? Will people notice my chipped tooth?*

When I entered, I was met with friendly welcomes. Nor could I detect any suggestion of concern or curiosity as we played bridge for the next two hours. I felt relieved. My inner self was clearly well-hidden with no disclosing cracks. My good spirits overflowed as I drove away.

But the next morning as I dressed for an appointment to play tennis with friends, I noticed that the bruising on my legs was now even more prominent. And I could hardly wear long pants to play tennis. *Some people wear nylons when they play. I'll put some on. I'll try some makeup too.*

After applying a liquid foundation to my legs, I pulled panty hose over them. Now I looked presentable, or so I hoped. Nancy, who had first suggested I attend the inner child workshop, was among the party of friends scheduled to play tennis with me that morning. When I reached the tennis clubhouse, she was already there. As we entered, I whispered to her, "Did you notice bruising on my legs?"

She looked down at my legs, horror flashing in her eyes. "What happened?"

I explained briefly. "But I'm okay. My concern is if the others will notice my bruising."

"Probably not," Nancy assured me. "If you hadn't called it to my attention, I probably wouldn't have noticed."

I headed towards the court. Would someone ask me why I was wearing nylons? If so, what would I tell them? But no one raised any questions as my friends and I volleyed balls back and forth. Then Donna, who was playing opposite me at that moment, gave me an up-and-down glance that settled on my legs. I held my breath. *Oh, no! She notices something. Here it comes!*

But Donna simply commented, "Cute tennis outfit, Sue. Turquoise looks good on you. It shows off your tan. It is new?"

I let out my breath in relief. "No, but thanks for the compliment."

After two sets of tennis, Nancy and I left. She gave me a hug. "You played a good game, Sue, and no one noticed your bruising."

"Yes, so long as I don't bring attention to myself, I'm fine." I returned Nancy's hug fervently. "You are such a good friend. You've stuck by me when others would have stepped out."

"Sue, I've known you many years. I know the behavior you've described isn't the real you." Nancy ran her hands through her hair. "I have to confess that I feel responsible, encouraging you to sign up for that inner child workshop. I wish you hadn't followed my advice."

I shook my head resolutely. "I'm glad you did. If there is some demonic force living inside me, then it needs to be looked at, dealt with, and conquered. Besides, once I leave the church, I am completely unaffected and my normal life resumes. Of course, having a friend like you who accepts me without judgement makes a big difference in helping me accept myself."

A few days later, we had another tennis match. Nancy met me in the parking lot before the game with a bag in hand. "Sue, I brought you some tiger balm for your neck and some holy water and rosary beads. From what you told me, it sounds like you're being demonically attacked. My aunt, who is a Catholic, has cast out demons in others. According to her, you put some of this holy water on your forehead and pray for Jesus' deliverance. You use the rosary beads to worship and praise Jesus."

Nancy handed me the bag. I shuddered as I looked inside and saw a small bottle of holy water, rosary beads, and tiger balm. No way would I use them!

Gaining control, I liberally applied the balm to my neck, feeling its soothing effect immediately. I threw the bag with its other contents in the back seat of my car. "Nancy, thanks so much for the balm. It's already helping."

I looked down at my legs. The bruising was lighter, but a little makeup was still necessary. *Don't give up! Time passes. Wounds heal.*

CHAPTER TWENTY-SIX

PROTECTION

The Lord will keep you from harm; he will watch over your life.

—Psalm 121:7

That night as I was preparing supper, the phone rang with a shrill jangle. I jumped. Larry answered it. "Honey, the call is for you. It's Father Allen."

I swallowed hard as I took the phone from Larry. *Is Father Allen cancelling our appointment for tomorrow? Am I too much for him?*

But Father Allen's voice sounded cordial. "Hi Sue. How are you?"

"Great! Couldn't be better," I responded. *I'll bet he doesn't believe me!*

"I'm calling because I think we might need more time tomorrow. Would you be able to stay at least two hours, maybe from 3:00 to 5:00 P.M.?"

"No problem. Whatever it takes, I'm willing to do."

But when I arrived again at the church, I was soon questioning how willing I really was. The first thing Father Allen did was hand me a large wooden cross. "We're going to start today with you holding this."

Immediately, that angry stranger I'd encountered inside me on my last visit emerged. Throwing the cross on the floor, it spoke in a gravelly voice. "I don't like crosses!" There were some Bible in the book case. "I don't like Bibles either." I said with a growl. My hand swiped across them. They fell on the floor, scattered as unpleasant discards.

Father Allen, Cleo, and Joan all began speaking in tongues, God's language that I didn't understand. Between gritted teeth, the angry stranger in me snarled, "What do you think you're doing? I don't like you or your crosses, Bibles, or Jesus. They revolt me. Make me sick."

Father Allen prayed over me in a commanding voice. "Leave Sue in the name of Jesus."

For an instant, calmness swept over me. Then the angry stranger was replaced with the witch-like one, and a harsh, sharp, cackle bellowed, "You think you're so smart, but you're powerless over me. I have control over Sue."

For the next two hours, Father Allen, Cleo, and Joan prayed over me, speaking in tongues and demanding the demon to leave. Meanwhile, I continued beating at my head and legs while making animal-like noises and postures. But when it was time to leave, I switched back to being normal me. How I could do this, I had no idea.

Over the following months, Father Allen, Joan, and Cleo didn't give up on me. One time they even resorted to working with me seven hours at a single stretch. By the end, Father Allen was red-faced with labored breathing and sweat pouring down his brow. I in turn left in shame that all their efforts had ended in failure. And yet I was still attending church with Larry and living a respectable life. Not just respectable, but a good life, enjoying my family, friends, and social activities.

Then one day Father Allen told me, "Sue, we could use additional assistance on this. Would you be willing to have these sessions at another church, just for a while?"

My heart plunged at his troubled tone. *As long as it's not my church, where I'm a respected member!* I blinked rapidly. "Sure, I'm not a quitter."

A week later, I had my first appointment at the new church with Rick, the assistant pastor. He began with casual conversation. "So tell me about yourself. Do you have a family?"

As I expounded on my good life—a loving, supportive family, good friends, healthy engaging activities—he lifted one brow. "So do you have a church life? Have you accepted Jesus as your Savior?"

At his question, anger erupted in me. What followed was a repeat of my sessions with Father Allen. As usual, once I left the church, I felt completely normal. I continued visiting Pastor Rick for several months with no improvement in my outrageous, out-of-control behavior. Besides my husband and Nancy, I'd told my two daughters, my sister Sandy, and several other good friends what was going on in my life. I'd braced myself for a reaction of shock and horror, but was relieved to see none.

By this time, the assistant minister Rick had become discouraged with my case. He brought in other spiritual leaders from his church, but nothing changed. Then one day he told me, "Sue, there's going to be a healer at our church next Saturday. She's well-known and has displayed miraculous gifts. Would you be willing to come and meet her?"

I was willing to do anything that might break this stalemate. The following Saturday, I arrived at Rick's church to find the sanctuary packed. As I found a seat at the back, an attractive, middle-aged Caucasian woman introduced herself as Norma Johnson. I learned that she was a very well-known Pentecostal ministry leader, pastor, speaker, and author on whom God had bestowed the gift of divine healing. I was intrigued, but doubted she could help me. After all, I didn't have a physical sickness or pain she could heal.

One by one, people came up to the platform. Placing her hands on them, Norma Johnson prayed for their individual needs—bad backs, ankles, knees, heart trouble, tumors. Touched by the Holy Spirit, each fell backwards and was lifted up quickly by a helping hand. They went back to their seats, convinced they were healed. I was astonished at how the healer seemed to sense and pinpoint their problem without being told.

But I had no intention of joining the action. In fact, what was I thinking to even come here? Was it curiosity, stupidity, or desperation? Just then, I saw Norma Johnson walking down the aisle towards me. My heart began to pound. *She isn't coming to talk to me, is she?*

Sure enough, Norma stopped by my pew. Putting her hand on my shoulder, she said, "You have a stinger in you that needs to be removed."

Her words triggered something in me. Jumping to my feet, I sprinted out of the church, heading toward the safety of my car. Rick and the senior pastor raced after me. Grabbing my flailing arms, they both yelled. "Sue, you're holding on to a sin. Confess. Only then will you find cleansing, forgiveness and redemption."

I began growling and hissing. In response, their voices grew in intensity. "Recognize your sin. Let it go. Pray for forgiveness and redemption."

Then somehow, I was my normal self again. Covering my face with my hands, I whimpered, "I haven't sinned. I haven't done anything wrong. Let me go. I want to go home!"

The two pastors finally released me and walked away, shaking their heads and muttering to themselves. As I drove away from the church, I felt crushed, in total despair. How could they accuse me of holding onto a sin, liking it, wanting it? After all, I went to church every Sunday. I kept my aversion against Christ to myself. I did church work. I tried to be a good person, cooperative and kind to everyone I met.

When I arrived home, Larry was watching television, his legs stretched out on the recliner. He looked up at me as I plopped down on the couch. "So what happened?"

"Well, I wasn't healed, that's for sure! The healer told me I had a stinger in me that needed to be removed. When I ran out, I was chased by two clergymen who yelled at me, accusing me of holding onto a sin."

Larry jumped up to sit next to me on the couch. "Sue, as I've said before, you've done nothing wrong. It's your family's fault. Who knows what they did to you! Or what trapped memories and feelings you've stuffed down inside."

With Larry's encouragement, my resolve came back, I knew what I had to do. Go back to the church. Explain myself. Seek deliverance. I called the next morning and asked the church receptionist to have Rick call me back. After anxiously waiting a few days, I called again and again. After several more tries, I had to accept that he didn't want to see me anymore.

I felt shocked and abandoned. How could a man of God betray me? Not want to help me? Did he think I was a bad seed with no chance for redemption? With no answer, I called Father Allen and asked if I could come back.

"Of course you can." Father Allen's voice was filled with compassion.

But the same torturous behavior continued at Father Allen's church. The prayer team was relentless—fasting, praying, laying on hands, speaking in tongues. I began to feel increasingly ripped apart by the forces of evil. I was also concerned for my two daughters. Could they have satanic influence in their life as I did? Reluctantly, both agreed to see Father Allen. I gave a sigh of relief when he found no sign of demonic oppression in either girl.

Larry remained concerned about my lack of progress. One day he came to me. "I've done some research, and from what I've learned, it would seem that when a person is demonically harassed, they've dealt at some point in their past in the occult, sexual sins, consuming hate, witchcraft, or black magic. You haven't, right?"

"Never!" I assured him vehemently.

He continued. "There has to be an open door that allows demonic harassment. Emotional neglect could also be the cause, or having undergone satanic abuse. Sue. There's no doubt you've been neglected. We've been married over thirty years, and your mother has shown no interest in being a part of our life. She lives twenty minutes from us and never even visits."

I shrugged. "I never really think about it. She's never been a part of my life. As to demonic influence, I don't believe that is my case. After all, I live a happy, successful life with a wonderful, loving family."

"You're right honey," Larry gave me a hug. "In fact, you're more normal than the normal—steady, someone who makes wise decisions, rarely raising your voice or getting angry."

I leaned into his hug, comforted, but silently, I thought, *You haven't seen my inner torture chamber.*

It was shortly before Christmas that year when I received a call from my stepfather Herman. Not long before, my mother had suffered a slight stroke. She'd recovered well, and in fact, I'd been pleased that the stroke seemed to have gentled her character, making her much softer and less critical in conversation. I'd even taken her on a Christmas shopping trip that turned out to be an unexpectedly pleasant outing with no harsh exchange of any sort.

"Your mother isn't feeling well," Herman explained when I answered the phone. "She won't be able to join you for the holiday get-together you are planning."

My first thought was that this was just another of Mother's excuses not to spend time with me and my family. But a few days later, Herman called again to say that Mother had passed away. After all I'd been through, it was hard to even process my feelings. Not long after her death, Herman contacted me to suggest I come over to his house and sort through her belongings.

I went right over. When I arrived, Herman handed me a sketchbook. "You might want to take a look at this. Your mother drew these."

I was stunned as I looked through the drawings in the sketchbook. They were ugly and frightening, the last one especially—a woman with huge biceps, bulging leg muscles, and enlarged hands that were gripping pitchforks. The woman's eyes were dark, narrow slits, her mouth an ugly scowl. Two horns curled up from her head gave her a demonic look.

The sketches took me back to the bizarre images I'd been grappling with all these years of my mother's face red and twisted in a demonic rage, burning crosses, coffins, and men in black cloaks. Was there any connection to those images and these sketches? Why had Mother drawn them? Had something actually happened I could not remember that would explain both my visions, Mother's horrible sketches, and my aversion to Jesus as well as my sister Sandy's?

Now that she was gone, there was no way for me to find out. I could only push it out of my mind like so much else. I put away the sketch book and didn't look at it again, concentrating instead on finding healing through my sessions with Father Allen and his prayer team.

One blessing during this time was the friendship I formed with Cleo, who was part of the prayer team. She became a healing balm in my life, accepting me, all of me, with trust and confidence. But my bizarre behavior during our prayer sessions didn't lessen even now that we were friends. I'd been meeting with the prayer team for deliverance a full year, often leaving Cleo, Joan, and Father Allen drained, puffy eyed, and red faced from exertion by the end of our sessions. There was nothing particularly different about the prayer session we were holding on August 5, 1995. But as the prayer team laid their hands on me and prayed, I experienced what felt like a lightning bolt run down my body. I opened my eyes wide. "What was that?"

"That was the Holy Spirit's indwelling Joan, Cleo and I have praying for," Father Allen explained.

I didn't really know what that meant, but I felt a glow inside and out that did not diminish as I drove home. *What's going on? Why do I feel this way?*

As soon as I stepped into my house, I felt an urge to read the Bible. After rummaging through drawers and shelves, I spotted one. Dusting it off, I opened the Bible. My eyes widened as I read the words to which the pages had fallen open.

> I waited patiently for the Lord: he turned to me and heard my cry. He lifted me out of the slimy pit, out of the mud and mire, he set my feet on a rock and gave me a firm place to stand
>
> —Psalm 40:1-3

I put my hand on my heart. *God is speaking to me! He has lifted me out of my troubled places. I am standing firm.* Throughout the rest of the day, that Bible drew me in like a magnet. I kept reading, thirsty for its teaching. As I reached the Gospels, which my aversion towards Jesus had always kept me from reading, I found myself amazed at the light, love, and wisdom revealed in Jesus Christ, the Son of Man.

I also encountered a strange word—Abba—repeating itself in my mind throughout the day. What did it mean? Could it be a biblical term? I found my answer in the New Testament epistle of Romans:

> The Spirit you received brought about your adoption to son ship. And by him we cry, *"Abba,* Father." The Spirit himself testifies with our spirit that we are God's children—heirs of God and co-heirs with Christ
>
> —Romans 8:15-16

But why Abba? It sounded like a foreign word. Wanting to understand further, I looked up the definition and found that it was an Aramaic word most closely translated as Daddy, conveying an intimate relationship and childlike trust. Only God, my Abba, my heavenly Father, could have implanted this word in my heart.

From the moment I was baptized in the Holy Spirit. On that day of August 5, 1995, my assurance of faith resonated in my heart. I was drawn to Jesus as my Savior, having absolute confidence from that day forward that I am His and He is mine.

CHAPTER TWENTY-SEVEN

SALVATION

The Lord is good to those who wait for him, to the soul who seeks him. It is good that one should wait quietly for the salvation of the lord.
—Lamentations 3:25-26

From the day Jesus became my Savior, my attitude changed from one who avoided reading the Bible, found it hard to understand and irrelevant to my daily life, to not being able to put it down. Cleo introduced me to the apologetics of C.S. Lewis. As she and I discussed the rationale of Jesus Christ's almighty power and the tactics of the Devil, I took it in eagerly and thirsted for more.

At just at this perfect time, Linda, my past neighbor and Christian friend, from whom I hadn't heard in years, called me. "Sue, would you like to join with me in a new Bible Study Fellowship (BSF) class? They are going to study Moses."

When she told me where the study would be held, I responded, "That's only a half mile from me! Remember when we went to BSF about thirty years ago? I dropped out because I didn't enjoy the lessons."

"I remember."

"Well, I had a born-again experience recently, and now I'm anxious to study the Bible."

I joined the BSF class. Studying the Word of Truth together with other believers, I found a unity in mind and thought, a common allegiance to the Lord Jesus and the gospel message. I also found a family of trust. In fact, this was the family I'd longed for all my life. A family that cared about each other and shared openly.

Winter turned to spring, the season that brings a burst of flowers poking up their heads from the thawing ground, dead-like branches sprouting green leaves, and birds building nests for their young. Just as life's revival was evident in nature, so the spiritual seeds Jesus was planting in my heart sprang to life. I was rejoicing in another new blessing as well as Larry and I made our final move into the same home where we still live today.

A beautiful three-thousand-square-foot house at the end of a steep, winding drive, our new home overlooked a picturesque mountain valley. The driveway was bordered by melaleuca trees, also known as paper bark trees, their leaves used for centuries as a calming tea. There was also an orchard of orange, avocado, peach, plum, and apple trees, promising sweet fragrance in the spring and mouth-watering fruit in the fall. Because of its panoramic view, we dubbed our home *Liston's Lookout*.

I now lacked nothing to complete my happiness. Yet during my continued prayer team sessions, I was still evidencing the same bizarre behavior. How could this be if Jesus had redeemed me and brought me into God's family?

A year after the prayer team had begun their weekly sessions with me, Cleo sought help from a Catholic church known for doing demonic deliverances. A deacon from their diocese obtained permission to attend my next session and observe my behavior. That morning as I drove to meet this stranger who might be able to deliver me from satanic power, a familiar sense of dread flooded my being. Memories surfaced of driving my father to a sanitarium, driving my assaulted daughter to a counselor, driving to see Dena in a mental ward for attempting suicide. Still, I hadn't turned back then, and I wasn't going to now.

Taking action conquers fear! I reminded myself, clenching my jaw with determination as I parked and headed into the church. When I reached the chapel where we always met, I spotted a tall, dark-haired stranger with the prayer team. Father Allen introduced him. "This is Bill, a deacon for the Catholic church. The bishop has recommended he work with you."

I shook the deacon's hand and took my usual seat in the chapel. That was when an explosion of angry emotions and bizarre behavior erupted. When I finally switched back to my normal self, my head hanging low in shame and embarrassment. His eyes filled with concern, Deacon Bill addressed me.

"Sue, I don't believe you are demon-possessed. Especially since you confess a personal faith in Jesus Christ. But you are definitely suffering from demonic oppression. More significantly, I believe that you have a multiple personality disorder. That means that your own core personality has split into multiple personalities, which are termed 'alters' or 'split personalities'. Some of your alters hate Jesus because they have not put their faith in him."

My body stiffened at his remarks. I felt insulted and furious. "I don't have a split personality. I'm normal. My life is good, happy, and stable. And I believe in Christ. My odd outbursts have nothing to do with this."

"What do you mean by alters?" Father Allen asked.

"It means Sue has a series of different personality states," Deacon Bill responded. "These hold the memories and past emotions that are too hard to handle in her normal daily life."

My face grew hot with anger. "Well, I'm not going to accept that I have a split personality. That sounds too weird! Sure, I know my past was dysfunctional, but I've handled it just fine. Ask my husband and kids."

Since Father Allen and the rest of the prayer team had been witnessing my bizarre outbursts for endless months, they could have pointed out the fallacies in my argument. But they held their peace, and Deacon Bill spoke up calmly, "Look, I'm not going to argue with you. But there's a Christian counselor I would like you to consider visiting. Her name is Dr. Marshall, and she is highly regarded for the work she's done with spiritual warfare and multiple personalities. I'll pay for your first visit."

I gritted my teeth. "Okay—just once."

Leaving the session, I headed to Barnes and Noble to look for a book on multiple personalities. I found *Uncovering the Mystery of MPD* (Multiple Personality Disorder) by Dr. James Friesen and bought it. But I wasn't ready to read it, so I just took it home and stuck it on a bookshelf. I was hesitant to mention the deacon's suggestion, but finally I told Larry, "Deacon Bill from the Catholic Church said that I have a split personality."

Larry shook his head. "I've never seen you show different personalities. In fact, you're always on a steady course—

organized, making healthy choices. This doesn't make sense."

"I agree. But Deacon Bill thinks I should go to this Dr. Marshall for further counseling. She specializes in multiples personalities that are infused with demonic activity. And Deacon Bill said he'd pay for the first session, so how can I refuse?"

"That sounds reasonable," Larry agreed. "I can't see how it would hurt, and if it might help, it's worth checking out. After all, with your sane, rational behavior and faith in God, I've never believed you are demon-possessed either. So there must be some other explanation for the behavior you've described at your prayer sessions. Maybe this Dr. Marshall can help find out what it is."

I was still not happy at the idea, but I made an appointment with Dr. Marilyn Marshall. As I drove up to a salmon-colored office building, I felt my head spin. *Dr. Marshall will be my fourth counselor. Will she be my last? How much more torment am I able to withstand?*

When I reached Dr. Marshall's office, I glanced at my watch. It was one my husband had given me, engraved with the inscription: *To My Love.* I was ten minutes early for my appointment. I peeked through a glass window in Dr. Marshall's door. I saw no one inside, so I let out a deep breath, opened the door, and stepped into her waiting room.

Inside, I heard the soothing sound of water trickling from a small table-top fountain. Along with a couch and high-backed chair, I could see a low shelf filled with children's books and games. A pink vase filled with dried flowers sat on a corner table. A sweet hint of jasmine scented the air.

The creak of a door to my left startled me. As I jerked my head around, a middle-aged woman with gray-streaked brown hair welcomed me with an outstretched hand and smiling, compassionate eyes. "Hi, I'm Dr. Marilyn Marshall. You must be Sue. I'm so glad to meet you. Before we get started, I have a few papers for you to fill out."

She handed me several papers on a clipboard. Once I'd filled them out, I followed her into her office. Walking over to a file cabinet, she placed my papers in a file. *How thick will that file become?* I wondered.

Picking up a note pad and a pencil, Dr. Marshall looked at me intently. "Are you comfortable?"

I shrugged. "Would you mind shutting the blinds?"

"Sure, no problem." Leaning over, she closed the blinds, then repositioned herself. "So tell me about yourself."

"Where do I begin?"

"What brought you here?"

I clenched and unclenched my hands. "I'm here due to a referral from Deacon Bill of the Catholic Diocese of San Diego. He accused me of having a split personality. Of course, I didn't believe him, but here I am. I'm not seeking counseling. In fact, I'm a very happy person with a close to perfect life. And just recently, we moved into the house of my dreams."

As I paused for breath, Dr. Marshall's eyebrows raised, "I see. Tell me more."

Words rushed out of my mouth. "Well, the deacon also witnessed my violent reaction to Bibles, crosses, and the mention of Jesus. At such times, something else like a stranger living inside me takes over."

"Yet you say you have close to a perfect life," Dr. Marshall commented mildly.

My hands turned clammy. "Well, yes. As soon as I walk out the door after my therapy, my life continues its happy beat. It's so strange. I don't understand it."

Picking up her pencil, Dr. Marshal wrote a few notes. I felt the rumbling deep within. As an outpouring of raw emotions spewed out, I threw myself down into the couch, face down. My insides felt like they were boiling. Wide, crazed eyes circled my head. Once again, I was seeing demonic faces, candles, crosses, blood, and burning stakes surrounded me. I gnashed my teeth and yelled out in despair.

Dr. Marshall was praying aloud, invoking God's power and the name of Jesus to cast out evil spirits. But her prayers only caused my symptoms to accelerate. A voice from deep inside me barked, "You can't pray for me. I don't accept God. And don't use the name of Jesus. He's evil himself. Don't ask me to hold that Bible on your desk either or the cross on your table. I'll throw them across the room. I don't like them."

I then morphed into the witch-like personality, cackling, "You can't help Sue. You're powerless."

After two hours of outbursts, Dr. Marshall said our time was up. As I came back to being me, I furrowed my brow. "How could I act this way? I'm a Christian. I believe in Jesus as my Savior and Redeemer. I even attend a Bible Study Fellowship class."

"Sue, you have a dissociative disorder," Dr. Marshall explained. "But you can actually consider it a gift from God. That disassociation has allowed you to survive emotional and spiritual abuse and leave it behind spiritually so that God's purpose might be fulfilled in you."

I was stunned. "Are you saying that I really do have multiple personalities? And that other personality is still open to demonic oppression even after I've accepted Jesus?"

"Yes. You've had past experiences that were just too overwhelming for you to deal with. So part of your mind reached out and encapsulated that painful memory until such a time as healing is received. Those parts of your mind can become different personalities that seem like a whole other person is inside you. We call those different personalities 'alters' or 'alternate personalities'. And they can emerge under certain stresses like your therapy sessions."

"Oh, that makes sense!" Instead of feeling distressed or angry, as I'd been when Deacon Bill brought up the possibility of alternate personalities, I found Dr. Marshall's explanation a wonderful relief. For the first time, I was being given hope that someone might be able to figure out what was wrong with me. And in that case, maybe Dr. Marshall could help me heal from my outbursts as well. "But it's so hard to accept that these alters are actually part of me and not some demonic presence as my other counselors have always told me."

"Well, we can talk about that next time." Dr. Marshal picked up her calendar from her desk and looked over her schedule. "Shall we make it next week same time?"

"Okay, sure," I agreed. "With God's help, I have the strength to face this reoccurring nightmare. And that's what it actually seems—not real at all."

"That's how dissociation works." Dr. Marshall walked me out to my car. "Drive carefully."

"Thanks, I will." I slid into the driver's seat, feeling lighthearted. God had clearly sent me to the right therapist. Turning the radio on high, I stepped on the accelerator, elated that I'd made it through another hurdle.

CHAPTER TWENTY-EIGHT

RESTORATION

For we are glad when we are weak and you are
strong. Your restoration is what we pray for.
—2 Corinthians 13:9

As I drove home, my mind slipped backwards into
the dark days of my childhood. I could now see
clearly the saving grace of God even then. When
I was in the depths of despair with Daddy in a
mental institution, strange men doing horrible things to me
in my own house, a mother who offered no protection or care,
God had sent me a next-door neighbor to become my
surrogate mother. She had showed me God's love, peace, and
power.

When I'd been forced to change schools in seventh grade,
feeling miserable, Louise had entered my life to become my
best friend and assure that God is my heavenly Father. Then
there was the incredible chance meeting when I was
seventeen of my future Christian husband, who set me on
the road of attending church every Sunday with his family.

And when God had set me on this journey into my
tormented mind, he'd also sent just the right people every

step along the way. Lisa, my first counselor, who'd helped my daughter Donna and then me, had been the first to bring me awareness of my dysfunctional family and inner pain. My Christian friend Nancy had led me to Dr. Miller, where the demonic influences on my life had been exposed. Father Allen, Cleo, and Joan had engaged in spiritual warfare on my behalf. And now God had led me to Dr. Marshall, an expert who treated dissociative disorders along with spiritual warfare.

Above all, God had at last led me to Jesus Christ, who had lifted me from the depths of despair, redeeming me through a born-again experience, assuring me of my salvation and the truth in God's Word. A smile lit up my face as I drove home, secure in the knowledge of God's guidance and protection in my life.

But my newfound peace and assurance did not signify that all my issues had now vanished. The very next week I returned to Dr. Marshall's office. I felt instantly relaxed at her welcoming smile, knowing I was in good care. Yet when I looked up at a framed picture saying "Save the Child and You Save Everything," there was a rumbling deep within.

"How has your week gone?" she asked.

"It was filled with fun-filled activities. Now I'm looking forward to going to Yosemite for a hiking vacation with my family."

"Sound like you enjoy your life," Dr. Marshall commented. "How do you feel about yourself?"

At her question, a feeling of intense self-hate filled my being. My jaw clenched. My arms lifted up and pounded me on my head. At least now I knew what was happening. One of my alternate personalities had emerged, an alter I came to call SELF HATE.

"She shouldn't have been born. Should be stepped on like a worm. Chopped up little pieces. She's disgusting, revolting.

Good for nothing. And her shoes are ugly. The earrings are too fancy." My earrings and high shoes were flung across the floor. "Who does she think she is? Miss Fancy?"

After SELF HATE had its say, an alter I call DARKNESS emerged, leaving me hunched over, head between my knees. Dr. Marshall queried, "Who are you?"

In a harsh sounding voice, the alter answered "I have no name. Not a real person. Just a miserable spirit, living in a dark hole, sinking in mire, with no escape."

The next hour was one of raw emotions lashing out, switching quickly, with no meaningful dialogue. I continued to return to Dr. Marshall each week. She would ask me about my background, and I told her about my dysfunctional family, Daddy's mental breakdowns, Mother's lack of interest, the renters who'd molested me.

"That must have been hard on you," Dr. Marshall commented.

I shifted in my seat. "Oh, I suppose so, but I managed fine. Never gave it much thought."

Her brown eyes looked deeply into mine. "What more can you tell me about your parents?"

"My father's mother died when he was only six months old. His father often kicked him out of the house to go live with his grandmother. But he was tough and worked hard to overcome obstacles. In high school he became a cheer leader and was named most likely to succeed of his senior class.

"And your mother?"

Feeling encouraged, I allowed my floodgates to open, nonstop. "Mother didn't seem real. Never had a friend visit. Kept to herself. I never knew her really. She was very smart, advanced two grades in school, and went to UC Berkeley on scholarships. But I always felt I didn't measure up to her. Daddy, Sandy and I tried to please her, but we never could."

"That must have been hard on you," Dr. Marshall responded. "So tell me more about your current life, how these alters are affecting you."

I blinked rapidly. "They don't affect me. I don't associate to them. They are not real. It's just like a movie I'm watching. My life couldn't be any better. I've always been a happy person."

Under her probing gaze, I admitted, "Well, that's not the whole truth. I've woken up heavy-headed and somewhat depressed every morning as far back as I can remember. But once I slip out of bed, my natural optimistic nature and busy schedule takes over."

At that moment, before I even realized what was happening, SELF HATE emerged and began pounding at my head. "I don't like Sue. I'll break her down, hurt her, and snap her neck. That's my job. I like evil, horror, and terror."

I plunged to the floor. Over the remainder of the session, other alters emerged, leaving once they'd had their say. When the session was over, Dr. Marshall walked me to my car again, making sure I was okay to drive home. I drove home, escaping into my normal, stable life. But I came back to Dr. Marshall time and again. I wasn't seeking counseling so much as I was a curious seeker looking for insight into my other selves.

Over the following sessions, other alters emerged, taking on with biting sarcasm the behaviors of my mother, sister, and even my aunt Margaret. ANGER, SELF HATE, and WITCH appeared again and again. I would shake and lash out, beast-like utterances coming from my mouth. Sometimes tough, brave animals emerged to protect my tortured inner child. A wolf that growled and showed its sharp teeth. A lion that showed its strong claws. A snake that hissed. A muscle-man bulging with strength and power. They appeared and left like a revolving door.

As with Father Allen's prayer team, I continued to react violently to the touch of a Bible or cross. When Dr. Marshall prayed in the name of Jesus, I grabbed the nearest couch pillow and covered my head, shaking.

In one of my lucid moments, Dr. Marshall asked me, "Do you have any idea how you became so against Christianity, how the demonic forces entered?"

My teeth clamped together. "I don't really know. But I can say that Mother hated Christianity. Her mother was a Catholic, and Mother used to say this showed ignorance and simplemindedness, especially the way her mother fondled her rosary beads while making absolutions every night. There wasn't a Bible in our house. She wouldn't allow it."

I went on, "I don't know what is real or not, but I have repeated visions of my mother with a red, demonic face, black, evil eyes, and a snarl that shows her teeth like a wolf. She was dangling a cross from her hand above my head and cackling. I once found a scrapbook of sketches she'd made."

With a shudder, I told Dr. Marshall of the horrible, demonic-looking woman that had been my mother's last sketch. "After seeing that, I decided she must have been truly evil. But her personality seemed flat. No emotions showed through. She appeared to be a shell of a person."

Dr. Marshall's expression held compassion "I'm so sorry. That must have been very difficult for you."

My eyes remained dry. "I didn't feel I was worth her notice since she treated me with no care or concern. Never asked about my school work, friends, or activities. But I've come to realize Mother had her own problems to bear. There was my father's mental illness, of course. But she was also consumed with her own phobias and anxieties. She was eventually diagnosed with an obsessive-compulsive anxiety disorder."

"And your father? You mentioned his mental illness."

"Daddy was a wonderful, loving father. We laughed together and played together. But he also had a manic-depressive disorder which would turn him into a crazed madman I didn't recognize. He was often locked up into a mental institution, sometimes for years."

I hunched my shoulders. "Still, my home wasn't bad. I never cried or felt sorry for myself. I had friends and enjoyed playing in the beautiful outdoors behind our house."

Dr. Marshall's eyebrows rose sharply. "Sue, you're in denial."

I knew she was right. As a child, I'd come to feel no pain or emotion. In my memories, I wasn't sad, angry, or upset, but simply accepted what was. Clearly, my dissociative disorder had carried my pain for me. But my continued reaction to Bibles, crosses, and the name of Jesus left me questioning the influence of demonic activity on the world and in myself. I began searching the internet for information. There were countless news articles that mentioned cannibalism, murder, mutilations, all in the context of Satanism. I read about cult groups that sacrificed victims as an offering to Satan. I also found advertisements of satanic Bible for sale.

By now I'd read Dr. Friesen's book, *Uncovering the Mystery of Multiple Personality Disorder*. It described how satanic abuse often accompanies a dysfunctional family like mine, which can open a door to dark forces that afflict the mind. What had happened in my own past to trigger such symptoms?

In our very next session, Dr. Marshall brought up the subject. "Would you allow me to have a priest come and do a deliverance? I know you are now a Christian, Sue, but some of your altered states are clearly still being strongly oppressed or controlled by demonic influences."

My hands remained calmly on my lap. "Of course. If you think it would help."

CHAPTER TWENTY-NINE

INDEFATIGABLE

The Lord shall fight for you; you need only be still.
—Exodus 14:14

D r. Marshall introduced me to Father James. I followed them into the office where Dr. Marshall and I had our sessions and went directly to my customary seat. I crossed my ankles and arms tightly as Father James explained, "I'm going to trace the sign of the cross over you and sprinkle you with holy water."

As he walked over to me, carrying a small bottle, I broke out in a rage and ended up writhing on the floor, hissing. This time it was WITCH who showed her teeth and claw-like fingers. I saw images of my father with crazed eyes and clenched fists, ready to attack me. Father James asked my alter for the names of demons, how long they planned to stay, and how they found an entry point. WITCH reacted by crawling to the back of a chair, hiding, banging my outstretched legs on the floor, and speaking in animal-like guttural noises. "I don't have to answer anything. I'm here to stay."

For the next several hours, Father James read Scriptures and said prayers for inner healing and deliverance, but with no results. Finally, he stopped. Opening my eyes, I switched in a split second to being me. As usual, my sweaty hair and clothes gave undeniable evidence to the war that Father James and Dr. Marshall had witnessed.

I clasped my hands together and looked down, ashamed. "I'm sorry I put you through such an abomination. It's beyond my control. Something I certainly didn't ask for."

"We know you're an innocent party," Father James answered gently. "Somehow, demonic entities have found entrance into your soul. We're here to command them to leave and stop tormenting you."

"But they aren't listening!" I wailed. "They won't leave. What have I done? I haven't dabbled in the occult. I'm not perfect, but I don't enjoy wrongdoing."

Dr. Marshall spoke up. "Sometimes alters act like demons, even though they're part of your own separated personality. They need understanding, help, and healing. They're also victims. Other influences are demons and need to be cast out. It's important to know the difference."

I was ready to go. I felt completely disconnected and independent from this horror film I'd just witnessed. Rising, I headed for the door. Dr. Marshall followed me. "See you next week same time?"

"Sure." I responded. "I may appear filled with evil. But God always rescues me. Thanks for your help."

But as I headed home, unwanted questions once again sliced through my mind. I loved Jesus with all my heart. I'd accepted him as my Savior. So how could such unsolicited behavior spring from that same heart? How long could I hold back all the hidden rage, anger, and distortions that came out now only in therapy? Maybe I was on my way to a full-blown mental breakdown. I could end up in a sanitarium like my father.

I'd arrived home when I received a phone call. "Hi Sue. This is Betty White, your Bible Study Fellowship (BSF) leader. Are you busy?"

My heart thumped against my chest. *Have I done something wrong? Does she sense my internal struggle?* But she asked cordially, "Sue, would you consider becoming a BSF leader?"

I was stunned at her request. I had only been in BSF for a year. What made them think I could be a leader? Still, I loved God. I loved the ladies in my class. I was eager to study the Bible. Yes, I had major battle scars lying deep within myself whose extent only God really knew. But I also had completely confidence that God would never forsake me. A thrill ran through my body that felt like an affirmation from God.

"Yes!" I told Betty White fervently. "I'll do it."

There was a momentary silence on the line. Then Betty said, "You might want to think about it, pray about it, talk to your husband first. I'll call back in couple of days."

I chuckled. "You're right, I suppose I should think about it. I know it's a lot of work. To be honest, I hadn't given that part a thought until just now."

As Betty had suggested, I consulted my husband. "Larry, I've been asked to be a BSF leader. They meet two mornings a week. There's a lot of homework. I'd have a class of up to sixteen ladies a week, with whom I'd have to follow up, see how they are doing, let them know I care. What do you think?"

As usual, he was immediately supportive. "If it's something you want to do, go for it. I'm not going to stand in the way of you serving God."

"It's God's will. I can feel it."

A month later, I found myself sitting among fifty other BSF leaders with my lesson and Bible in hand. I looked over the group. Varied ages, hair styles, and attire, but all neatly dressed in their Sunday best. My navy-blue blazer and matching skirt with a white blouse seemed appropriate. I sat up straight, feeling I belonged.

Then the unexpected occurred. When the Bible study referenced Jesus, my insides vibrated in upheaval, ready to erupt. Holding it in with sheer determination, I closed my eyes, an image forming in my mind of running to the center of the room, throwing my body down on the floor, beating my head, snarling like a wild dog. I prayed desperately, "God, rescue me!"

The upheaval disappeared as fast as it came. Glancing around the room, I spotted no looks of concern or disapproval directed my way, so clearly no one had noticed my reaction. Picking up my lesson notes with trembling hands, I continued on with the Bible study.

Satan is trying to ruin my life, shatter my soul, I told myself firmly. *But it's not working. God fills me with His love. Jesus is my unmerited Savior. The Holy Spirit who is my helper abides in me.*

With a renewed sense of inner strength, I drove home. By now, I'd already skimmed through Dr. James Friesen's *Uncovering the Mystery of MPD* (Multiple Personality Disorder), which I'd purchased when I was first diagnosed with this disorder. At that time, I'd felt that description didn't fit me. It was easier to admit I was demonically oppressed.

Now, after years of it pounding me on the head, I had to accept the truth that the description of a multiple personality fit my behavior perfectly.

Picking up the book, I fell into the nearest seat and opened it. A licensed psychologist and minister, Dr. Friesen was considered a pioneer in the treatment of multiple personality and dissociative disorders. I glanced through the book's table of contents, which included mentions of spiritual warfare, satanic ritual abuse, as well as the diagnosis, characteristics, and treatment of MPD.

Among aspects mentioned were that distinct parts of the personality controlled the behavior of someone with MPD. These are involuntary and function independently. One paragraph explained how dissociation is actually a positive characteristic, since it permits the person with MPD to separate instantaneously from their memory of a painful event. Rather than being burdened by the degrading or traumatic memory of awful events, their self-image is protected.

That sure sounds like me! I realized. *I haven't been troubled by my past. Maybe I should be grateful instead of fighting against releasing the frozen horrors of my past? But why do I act out in such hate for myself if this has resulted from something I didn't do? Why do animal-like personalities lash out from me as though I'm not human? Why are the demons, real or imaginary, trying to destroy my life and my mind? What terrible things happened that I don't remember? It doesn't make sense!*

I read through Dr. Friesen's list of characteristics normally found in a person with MPD. High intelligence, high creativity, a high ability to use imagery, an inappropriate need to please, an urgency about life and time. Yes, those descriptions fit me well enough. Maybe I should feel flattered I had a few worthwhile attributes that contributed to creating alternate personalities.

More pertinently, if these alters were doing their job, keeping my inner turmoil out of my everyday life, then I needed to understand them, not fight against them. I decided on a trip to the library to do some research. When I arrived there, I shuffled through the card catalogue. I felt my face flush as I landed on the category of *mental dysfunctions*. Still, I jotted down the Dewey Decimal numbers and headed to that section of the library. It took hours before I finally found what I wanted. Sitting at the nearest table, I began reading.

"At a young age, your brain forms neural pathways, setting up long-standing habits and personality traits and mapping a great deal of information for life-long use. Stress, ability, and a young age combine to allow some people to create alternate personalities—other people who share the same body, but can have different emotions, thoughts, skills, and interests. This can be life-saving for a person who continues making alters, permitting them to deal with abuse while maintaining a normal life and holding onto needed relationships."

Putting the book down, I rested my head between my hands. It all made sense now. My next step would be to talk to my therapist about these various compartments of my mind, what they'd done to save my life, and why they were still here. After all, I had a normal life now. A secure life. A happy life. So their role should be over.

CHAPTER THIRTY

OWNERSHIP

For all who are being led by the Spirit of God, these are sons of God.

—Romans 8:14

T he days rolled by, and I found myself back in Dr. Marshall's office. My head resting back on a pillow, I told her, "I still don't understand how I can have different personalities living inside me. After all, except for during therapy, I don't have mood changes or unusual behavior. I live a well-balanced life."

Instead of offering an explanation, she asked, "Why do you think this is so?"

I paused to organize my thoughts. "Well, some of it is beginning to make sense. My fragmented personality deals with the abuse I experienced as a child. Though I never thought of myself as mistreated. I guess I didn't know the difference, so I thought of my life as normal."

"Yes, your alternate personalities have been a life-saving device," Dr. Marshall agreed. "You kept your anguish sealed in a mental lock-box so you could keep reacting to your caregivers in a normal way."

"That's true," I admitted.

"So how would you describe your mood as a child?"

"Good. I had fun, played in the canyon, enjoyed every flying and crawling creature, and found friends who accepted and liked me. I always felt appreciative for having plenty to eat and a roof over my head."

Dr. Marshall smiled warmly. "You have a good attitude."

I shrugged. "Trying to avoid problems just comes naturally."

"Do you still feel responsible for other people's feelings?"

I nodded. "Yes, I do my best to bring a smile, a lightness of heart. You could say that I'm a peacemaker."

"And can you see now that your emotions are stored in these alternate personalities?"

I nodded again. "That makes sense. Displaying emotions wasn't safe in my house. It was a sign of craziness, being out of control."

My mouth felt suddenly dry. My insides began to rumble, mental anguish filling my soul as I threw myself face down on the couch. My eyes clamped shut. My face became distorted. Different voices and personalities came and left in rapid succession.

This behavior continued month after month, which turned eventually into years, as I kept on pursuing into the darkness of my mind. After ten years of therapy with Dr. Marshall, I could hold the Bible without adverse reaction, read Scriptures, speak of Jesus, and hold a cross in my hands. My various injured parts would stay out longer during our sessions, allowing Dr. Marshall to administer therapy and healing. Animals no longer appeared for protection. My inner children felt safe to reveal their various personality states of terror, denial, or strength.

When I mentioned discontinuing therapy to my family and a few friends, they concurred. "You've always seem fine to me. I never understand why you went in the first place. It brings out torture you don't need, don't deserve."

I bit my lower lip. *They're right. It's time. I've made many winding turns, traveled down a lot of beaten paths, and now I'm caught in a cul-de-sac, blocked from any forward motion. I no longer see any possible forward motion.*

When I told Dr. Marshall, she pressed her lips together. "Are you sure you want to quit? You're doing much better, but there's still more work to do."

I stood firm. "You've been so kind to me. But it's time."

Dr. Marshall's eyes were searching, but kind. "The decision is yours. Just remember, my door is always open."

"Thank you." I left without turning back, enjoying the fresh air and singing birds that seemed to be giving me their seal of approval. After so many years, I no longer felt a need to open up and explore my personality. I accepted that Jesus' name still brought a rumbling deep inside, but I carried on, knowing that I loved my Savior, and worked on living my life in such a way that would reflect Jesus to others. I continued on as a BSF leader, confident that I was fulfilling God's purpose for me.

Two years rolled by. These included the blessing of twin grandbabies born October 10, 2004, as well as our two older grandkids, ages three and four when the twins were born. Sitting on the rug, bouncing them on my knees, acting silly and crazy, watching them laugh brought me a childlike carefreeness I hadn't experienced in my own childhood. An adoring husband, grown daughters who were also my best friends, hobbies of yardwork, tennis, and bridge all kept me happy and involved. These were my ropes of life to which I hung on to for my security and stability.

Then a bomb exploded—not literally, but mentally and emotionally. A girlfriend of mine had a son, Matt Baglio, who was a journalist. She told me about a book he'd written called *The Rite*, which chronicled exorcisms he'd witnessed in Rome. I wanted to read his book in order to learn more about demonic influences, their power, and how an exorcism can extract evil spirits. Obtaining the book, I began reading it during a family vacation with grandkids lying on the carpet, playing with blocks and tinker toys. Immediately, Satan's face formed in my mind—red faced, throbbing veins, a mouth of sharp, long teeth. Sweat began to form on my brow. My jaw clenched, and my fists knotted.

Running into the bathroom, I locked the door and sat on the toilet while I repeatedly slapped my head with full force. A creepy, evil voice manifested itself, saying, "You're a mess, Sue, no good, worth less than a worm." I was consumed with hate for myself. A force threw me down on the tile floor writhing, arms flailing.

While this was not unusual during my therapy sessions, it had never happened before at home during my "normal" daily life. Somehow, I returned to my customary sane self and joined my grandkids on the carpet. Larry, my two daughters, and their husbands came in from the pool, and we enjoyed a pleasant lunch together. The rest of our vacation was equally enjoyable with no more of the bizarre experiences that had sent me into the bathroom. But I knew I had to call Dr. Marshall, tell her about my experience reading *The Rite,* and ask her if I could come back.

When I called, Dr. Marshall sounded pleased. "I told you we weren't finished. I have an opening next week."

I felt warmed all over as I walked into her office and heard her welcoming voice. But when I explained the reason I was there, my temper exploded and my self-hate erupted into hitting, name calling, and strange voices. I was shocked, but knew more work needed to be done. I could only lose by giving up, right?

I continued therapy for two more months, but with no improvement. My sleep was affected, and I went back to sleeping pills and drinking. Finally, a sleep psychiatrist was able to help with my insomnia. I knew Dr. Marshall was very good, experienced, knew the right techniques. But I also felt we were no longer making any progress. I stopped my sessions with Dr. Marshall, certain God would lead me in the right direction at His right time, just as He had in the past.

Feeling a calling from God, I began leading a Bible study at a rehabilitation center called El Cajon Transitional Learning Center, or ECTLC, which is about a ten-minute drive from my home. The center reaches women who have suffered from drug addictions, prostitution, self-mutilation, prison, and suicide attempts. The invitation to teach a Bible study there came through from a wonderful Christian woman named Ruth Benson, who gives of her time and self to help these women. When I arrived for the first Bible study, I could see suspicion on the faces of the women crowding the center's small meeting room. But as I expounded eagerly on Scriptures that spoke of forgiveness through accepting Christ and the possibility of a fruitful, meaningful life, their suspicion changed to hope. Over time, the women began finding healing, faith in Jesus Christ, and trust in the Bible as God's inspired Word.

I could relate to them. God had lifted me up in my dark places. He had protected me. He'd given me hope and a guiding force. As I witnessed their distrustful, wary eyes take on a glow when the Bible was opened up to them, I felt richly blessed. God's hand was on my life. His Presence was in my heart. And now I was experiencing the honor and privilege of sharing the precious gift from God that I'd received with others who needed them as much as I did.

CHAPTER THIRTY-ONE

GIFTS

Each good and perfect gift is from above, coming down from the Father.

—Hebrews 4:16

One year later, I felt an intense desire to share my gratitude with Ruth Benson for the opportunity she'd given me to teach God's Word. Rummaging through a drawer of papers and cards, I found a card on which she'd written her phone number. When I called her, she seemed as pleased to hear my voice as I was hers. We met a week later for lunch at a local Italian restaurant. Over pizza, I spilled forth my crazy life of demonic warfare and split personalities.

Ruth reached across the table, placing her hand on mine. "Sue, have you received the help you need?"

"I've had years of counseling," I responded. "My demonic assaults have lessened. I can now hold a cross and the Bible. But the image of Jesus in my head is still deranged, like the devil himself. And I still don't like the name of Jesus. It stirs a disturbing rumbling from deep within my core."

"The reason I'm asking is because I've worked with people who have been demonically oppressed," Ruth went on to explain. "It's often not due to any fault of their own."

At that moment, Ruth began speaking in tongues. As she did so, it seemed to me that she was surrounded by an ethereal glow, as if she'd transcended into a spiritual realm. As she spoke, I held my breath in awe. After a few minutes, she stopped and spoke to me directly. "I get so emotional when God speaks to me. God told me it's your mother's fault."

My mouth hung open. "How did you know that? I haven't told you anything about my mother, but it makes sense."

She looked at me closely. "I know someone who could help you. Are you interested?"

"Yes!" I responded fervently. "My mind still holds mysteries that need to be solved."

"Then I'd like to recommend Nathan Daniel. He holds a master's degree in divinity, has been a pastor for thirty five years, and ministers internationally to pastors and missionaries. He specializes in training others to do exorcisms as well as doing deliverances himself."

"This is amazing!" I responded. "Time and time again, God puts just the right people in my path. Look at you, bringing my ECTLC Bible study into my life, which has been such a pleasure and joy. And you've affirmed through the voice of God that Mother is the reason behind my mental monsters. Now you know of someone who could help me, just at the right time when I've been looking for additional help."

Ruth picked her purse off the floor. "And that's not all. Just when I was leaving my house, I felt prompted to throw my address book in my purse." She dug out the book with a big smile. "Here is Nathan's phone number."

I wrote down the number. "Hey, he has the same prefix as me. Do you know where he lives?"

"Yes. In Harbison Canyon. Not far from me."

My head spun. "Really! I live ten minutes from Harbison Canyon. I must live close to you too. Divine providence is definitely at work here."

As soon as I returned home, I called the number Ruth had given me. A man's voice responded. "This is Nathan Daniel. How can I help you?"

"My name is Sue Liston," I told him. "Ruth Benson advised me to call you. She thought you might help me with some disturbances I'm having—possible satanic attacks."

"Sure, I'd be happy to see you," he said. "In fact, someone canceled an appointment with me for tomorrow at 10:00 a.m. Can you come then?"

Thank you, God! I breathed heavenward before responding, "I'll be there. Thanks for seeing me so soon."

The next morning, I drove to the address I'd been given, feeling confident to face my fears again with God's protection. When I reached the address, it turn out to be a two-story house painted light yellow with white shutters. I rapped on the front door. The door opened to reveal a man around fifty-five years old, slightly built with thinning hair and a well-trimmed beard.

"I'm Nathan Daniel." He offered me a handshake. "You must be Sue. Please come in."

I followed behind him into a room tucked in the corner of his house. I was startled to find Ruth Benson there with another woman I'd never met. Nathan gestured to Ruth's companion. "I'd like to introduce you to Jeanette. We work as a team."

Jeanette gave me a wide smile accompanied by a firm handshake. I took a seat on a couch as the two women settled themselves in chairs a few feet from me. Looking over at Ruth, I stated with a question in my tone, "You didn't tell me you'd be here."

"I told you I work with people who are demonically oppressed when I gave you Nathan's telephone number," Ruth explained. "He is the person I work with. I often help Nathan cast out demons."

My shoulders slumped. "Oh!" Nathan asked, "Do you mind if I record you?"

"No," I replied in a gruff voice that I didn't recognize.

I answered questions between clenched teeth. Then in a split second, an angry alter burst from me. Our session lasted over an hour with me pounding, stomping my feet, and speaking in a voice that wasn't mine. When I came back to myself, I offered my apologies. Nathan gave me a CD that contained a copy of the recorded session. As I walked out with it, I already felt detached from the other person inside me. With the recording gripped tightly in my hands, I couldn't deny the reality of my other self. But I wasn't ready to listen to it now. I placed the recording behind a stack of other CDs in the family room.

Nathan called me at few days later. "Hi, Sue. This is Nathan Daniel. How are you?"

I cleared my throat. "Believe it or not, I'm doing great. Just great. Be assured, I've been experiencing such outbursts for years. But I just leave them behind and resume my good life. Do you think you can help me?"

"Look, I mainly focus on the demonically possessed," Nathan responded. "I've given your behavior a great deal of thought. What I saw and heard was clearly not you. But I think we're dealing here with a split personality, not demons. And that is an area where I don't have experience."

"How can you be so sure it wasn't a demon?" I asked anxiously.

"Well, another personality speaking through your mouth and controlling body movements could be a demon. But what you displayed spoke rationally, upholding and defending your position in life. Demons aren't there to help us cope, but attempt to drive us to insanity, intent on destroying our lives. They don't dialogue or communicate, but only lash out in rage and hate. Didn't your counselor address any of these issues?"

I explained how Dr. Marshall had worked with me, relying on God's power, Scripture, and prayer. "Much of my demonic oppression has lifted, but as you can see, I still need help."

"If you'd like, I'll try to find someone else to help you."

"Oh, yes, thank you!" I responded fervently.

Nathan's offer left me hopeful, but another couple weeks slipped by without a return call. One day I was outside pruning roses, when Larry walked over to me, my CD from Nathan Daniel's session in his hand.

"What's up?" I asked.

"I'm just wondering if you've ever gotten around to listening to this CD."

I shook my head decisively. "No, I'm afraid to."

Larry took my hand. "Well, I think maybe it's time. How about if I listen to it with you."

Taking off my gardening gloves, I followed Larry into the house. I made myself comfortable on the couch while Larry inserted the CD in the player. The first words I heard were an alter I call PROTECTOR exploding out of me with a bombastic voice. "She is God-directed. She is protected by God. She's a Stephen's minister at her church where she uses her caring skills to help people in need. She's a Bible teacher. Has respect."

Larry, who had taken a seat beside me on the couch, nudged me, "It sounds like your split is a spokesman for you. Not your enemy at all."

I nodded, "That's true. I'm surprised it defends me with such passion."

On the CD, Nathan was continuing his interrogation. "Are there demons there?"

PROTECTOR answered. "How do I know? I'm not a demon."

"Are you a split?" Nathan was now asking.

"Dr. Marshall thinks I am." My voice on the CD sounded agitated. "She gave me a personality test. I'm very introverted. Sue's very extroverted. I don't trust people. Sue does. She's told nine people about her split personality. That's pretty trusting, don't you think? Besides, I keep my eyes shut. Sue wouldn't consider talking to someone with her eyes shut. But you know what? I don't trust the reaction all my junk would have on an observer. I couldn't stand the look of horror in their eyes. I'm crazy, weird, right? You don't have to answer that."

Heavy breathing and pounding could be heard.

"Are you angry? Do you feel hate toward anyone—like your mother?"

"No!" I shouted.

Jeanette asked, "Sue's never been angry?"

"That's not reasonable to ask," PROTECTOR said. "Of course, she's been angry. But she lets it go," More hitting and heavy breathing blasted through the recording.

"Speak the truth. Be angry, then forgive," Nathan Daniel said. "When you are angry, you form a splinter that gives energy for a demon to enter. In my past as a minister, I've experienced chronic pain and lustful thoughts. When I realized that I was carrying anger, I released it and was healed."

Nathan kept on. "You've been neglected. You have self-anger stemming from your childhood. You're enjoying it, holding onto it."

Shifting in my seat as I listened to the recording, I looked over at Larry, "He could be right. I've always blamed myself for not deserving love or care. The past pain, suffering, and anger could be held in my split personality. My emotions seem frozen in time."

"Why are you here?" Nathan was now asking my alter.

PROTECTOR responded. "When Sue was little, she was defenseless, scared, couldn't express, would be thrown in a sanitarium. I don't know! Still, Sue kept her feelings hidden, was able to leave home and face the world with a smile on her face."

Nathan cleared his throat. "Outside, calm. Inside, angry." He paused, then went on, "Sue has Jesus. Can Sue tell you to leave?"

"Sue doesn't have control over me."

"How are you helping Sue now? You must be here because she wants you to."

I could hear the resounding sounds of my hands slapping my head. Then Ruth's voice asked, "Are you angry at yourself?"

"I like to hit Sue. It feels good. I'm not human. Don't conform. I can do what feels good."

"Does Sue enjoy this?" Ruth asked.

"Yes—a release," PROTECTOR answered.

"Why?" Now it was Nathan's voice answering.

"It sets Sue free from overwhelming emotions," PROTECTOR said.

Nathan voice thundered. "That isn't your friend. It's darkness. Not Jesus, or God- directed."

Larry and I listened until the recording finished. Then I looked at Larry beseechingly. "I need to read through Dr. Friesen's book on multiple personalities again. There's so much I don't understand."

Larry nodded, "Me neither. I've lived with you for over half my life. You're more normal than anyone I've ever met—level-headed, balanced, and emotionally stable."

"Then why does this protector feel a need to defend me?" I responded, confused.

Larry looked thoughtful. "Maybe because you've always tried to please others, not stick up for yourself."

"Well, that's true," I admitted with a deep sigh. "I've always felt others are more important than me."

CHAPTER THIRTY-TWO

DIRECTION

By day the Lord went ahead of them in a pillar of
cloud to guide them on their way and by night in a
pillar of fire to give them light.

—Exodus 13:21

Several more weeks had passed when Nathan
called again. "Hi Sue. This is Nathan. I have
good news. After checking around for a
therapist qualified to handle your case, I
touched base with Dr. Friesen."

My jaw dropped with surprise. "Really! I have his book,
*Uncovering the Mysteries of MPD (Multiple Personality
Disorder)*. He's considered a pioneer in the treatment of
multiple personalities."

"Good, then you know how well qualified he is. And his
recommendation is that you see Mrs. Margie Alvarado, a
Christian counselor who has a great deal of experience
working with multiple personalities and demonic
disturbances. She lives in Vista. Is that too far for you to
drive?"

Vista is a city about forty miles north of San Diego. "I'd consider going to Timbuktu for help!" I responded with a chuckle. "Driving to Vista is no problem at all."

Nathan gave me a phone number for Margie Alvarado, and I called it without wasting any time. A woman's voice answered the phone. When I explained my called, she said pleasantly, "Oh, yes. Dr. Friesen told me you were going to call."

Margie Alvarado turned out to be smartly-dressed, attractive woman with dark-brown compassionate eyes and a friendly personality. I instantly liked her. Once I'd filled out the usual forms, I asked her, "Margie, would you mind if I record our sessions? The minister who last worked with me recorded our time together. It was very helpful."

"That's a good idea," she nodded.

I took out a digital recorder, placed it on a side table, and turned it on. Then Margie began asking about my background, childhood, hobbies and interests. I filled her in about my current good life as wife, mother, and grandmother. But when I began sharing about my dysfunctional childhood and my many years of counseling, a rage within me boiled over and exploded.

"Sue thinks she does everything right!" SELF-HATE yelled in a guttural voice, slapping my head over and over again. "She just got back from vacation, has too many frills. Just floats around. Thinks she's perfect. I can't stand her. She's empty headed, vacuous, worth nothing."After releasing emotions of overwhelming self-loathing, my mind switched to an alter I call CALM. Uncrossing my legs, it sat back into the couch.

"Who are you?" Margie asked.

"I don't know."

"How do you feel?" Margie asked.

"I have no feelings."

Then another alter called ANGER appeared. It balled up its fists, punched the couch, and gritted its teeth.

"Are you Sue?" Margie asked.

ANGER shook its head back and forth. "No."

"How do you feel?"

"I'm so angry."

"Why are you so angry?" Margie asked patiently.

"I'm a mess."

"You don't care about Sue?"

ANGER nostril's flared. "I'm beyond help."

Then DENIAL appeared. Staring straight ahead, DENIAL told Margie, "I have no feelings. Nothing can hurt me. I'm blank like a wall without any pictures."

"What do you know about Sue?" Margie asked.

DARKNESS suddenly switched in, burying its head in a pillow. "I live in a black hole. My mind is black too. Sue's not like me. I mess her up."

My various alters seemed frozen in time, switching constantly and rapidly between SELF HATE, CALM, ANGER, DARKNESS and DENIAL. Over the following year of weekly counseling sessions, Margie patiently gave each alter respect and compassion, while they each processed their pain. Finally, changes began. The different splits stayed out longer, which allowed Marge to get to know them and administer therapy.

As I listened afterwards to the recordings, I heard SELF HATE explode and hit my head repeatedly. "Who does Sue think she is? Talking, talking, and more talking. That's all she does. I've had it with her. She's trash, has a vacuum head, good for nothing."

"Why do you hate Sue?" Margie asked SELF HATE. "She has a good life."

CALM emerged. "Why would I hate Sue? I don't get involved in her life. That's her business. She does her best."

"Isn't it sad there's a part of Sue that holds her pain and suffering?" Margie responded.

After a few deep breaths, CALM answered, "I can visualize Sue's eyes, crazed, having a breakdown like her father. But that doesn't bother me."

"Tell me more."

"Okay, I can hear the screen back door opening as well as the front door at odd hours of the night, letting strangers in. I was alone, downstairs. Mother was upstairs, but didn't care about me. When I told Mother I was afraid of her renter, she ignored my fears. And when they molested me, she ignored that too."

Margie's eyebrows lifted. "You have awareness."

"Yes, but no feelings are attached."

"What do you long for?" Margie asked.

"Peace. But let's talk about the flowers in the vase on your shelf. Are they real?"

"We can talk about that, but I'd rather talk about you."

CALM avoided Margie's gaze. "I have nothing to say. I'm just a voice. But I can visualize that I'm at the beach. A bird flies over. I hold onto its wings and take flight over the mountains and down a rainbow. Now I'm a colorful fish painted in a rainbow of colors swimming the deepest ocean. The water is cool, refreshing."

CALM's mouth curved into a smile. "Now I'm flying over the tallest mountain on the wings of an angel."

DENIAL switched in, sounding confused. Margie asked, "Who are you?"

"A small dot of nothingness. I don't have a name."

"You're denying your existence," Margie pointed out.

DENIAL took a deep breath. "I'm not here, not real."

"What do you think of what Sue's wearing?"

"She's wearing a green shirt and black pants."

"Do you like it?"

DENIAL shrugged. "It's okay."

"Tell that to Sue."

"I can't tell her," DENIAL said flatly. "She's not here."

"Who are you?" Margie asked again.

"I'm not."

"You share space with Sue."

"I have no substance. No body."

It was in my second year of therapy with Margie that a new alter switched in, which I called SENSIBLE. This alter appeared open-minded and tried to make sense out of the senseless. Yet SENSIBLE needed to be between four walls, explaining that it wasn't strong enough to go outside, but wanted to figure it out what its purpose was.

"You need to acknowledge and work on your hidden pain," Margie told SENSIBLE with a quiet voice. "I know you and Sue want to be healed. What if God gave you a key and you could open a closed door where there's somebody who knows something?"

SENSIBLE began stepping towards the imaginary door when WITCH materialized. Turning its hands into claws, WITCH cackled, "You are powerless. Can't do a thing to help Sue."

A split called DARKNESS took over. "It's not pleasant to be me, filled with dark, distorted anger. I'm torn inside out. I have a monster face, dark, gnashing teeth—people would hate me. I'm distorted. Evil. Junk. Have to hide self. I'm anti-social. Guts exposed. Not pleasant what's revealed."

Margie's voice sounded soft and gentle. "God wants you healed."

ANGER hit me over my head and pounded my legs. "Why does God want to bother with me? Besides, I like who I am and my other parts like being out, airing feelings kept hidden for so long."

I was still also grappling with recurrent distorted images of Jesus. But at least the prior images I'd had of being in a coffin, seeing burning crosses, and chanting people in black robes had not returned since my time with Dr. Marshall. When I told Margie about the images, she explained, "The images could be from something you witnessed as a child or that happened to you that you can't remember. But they could also come from alters who've been demonically influenced or even from actual demons who have deliberately inserted such horrible images into your mind. Let's talk about the distortions you've described visualizing Jesus."

"I still have them, but they don't bother me. I know that isn't how Jesus looks. It's a miracle that with my distortions, I can still teach the Bible to a Christian rehabilitation center, be a leader in Bible Study Fellowship, and minister to lonely people. I'm a simple person, amazed God's using me in so many ways. Some of the people I minister to even say they love me. That's even more amazing."

Margie looked surprised at my last statement. "Do you know what love is?"

I raised my shoulders. "I know my father loved me."

"Did he ever hurt you?"

SELF HATE switched in again, clamped its eyes shut, balled its fists, and let out fierce growling while hitting my head repeatedly. Margie addressed SELF HATE sternly. "Sue has a good life.".

"Sue's a mess! Look at her eyes. They're crazy like her father's."

Margie began praying aloud. "Oh, Lord. I know you are the healer. Sweep this up. Lift it up. Remove it."

As SELF HATE buried its face in a pillow, Margie encourage, "Don't hide your face. You have nothing to hide from. You don't have to live like that anymore. Recognize who you are. Appreciate who you are. Be comforted."

CHAPTER THIRTY-THREE

GOD'S HAND

So do not fear; for I am with you; do not be dismayed, for I am your God. I will strengthen you and help you; I will uphold you with my righteous right hand.

—Isaiah 41:10

It wasn't until my third year of counseling with Margie that LITTLE SUE felt safe to reveal herself. She emerged with slumped shoulders and quivering lips.

"No one can hurt you," Margie told her softly. "God is protecting you, drawing you to Him. He wants you to be happy. I believe that. He wants that for you."

LITTLE SUE's eyes welled up. She whimpered. "No, I'm a mess, evil, apart from God."

"You're not evil."

"Yes, I am. If God loves me, why isn't He taking away my misery?"

"Let's do nothing but be," Margie said with a gentle voice. "I will ask God to bring light in, okay?"

Over the following months, Margie's office became like a womb, allowing my inner child to have a rebirth from a damaged past as well as a soft pillow to expound on my daily life. She asked if I ever get angry.

"There's not much to get angry about," I chuckled. "Of course, there are obstacles along my path, but they are usually smoothed over, resolved, or ignored. Solving the mysteries of my mind has been the steepest climb in my life. Sometimes I crawl as I go, but there really is no choice."

"Really? You don't think you have a choice?"

"No, I do what needs to be done. My mind over my heart, I guess."

She looked probingly into my eyes. "How are you accepting your alters?"

My fingers interlocked. "I realize they hold my buried pain, but it's so hard, accepting something so foreign to myself."

"You know you have walls. How would you feel if the walls break down?" Margie went on encouragingly, "Let's look at your alters. Ask them to come out."

"That's not up to me," I responded quickly.

"Because? Are you afraid of losing control?"

I looked away from her gaze. "I don't know."

"Do you feel the alters trust you?"

My face felt flushed. "Again. I don't know. I have no idea. We don't communicate with each other. There is no relationship. Only you can talk to them."

"Are you ready to communicate with them?"

"No."

"Are you ready to reach out to them?"

I folded my arms across my chest. "What do you mean by that?"

242

With steady gaze, Margie answered, "To have a relationship with them."

Sudden tension tightened my neck muscles. "I'm afraid of them. I want them separated from me. That's where I want them to be. If they came out in my life, I would lose control. My life would come crashing down, upsetting all my good work and effort."

With no letup, Margie countered, "So you do need control."

I was quiet for a dozen heartbeats before I answered, "They need to have control over themselves. As I've said, I have nothing to do with it."

"What if you could reach out to them so that they would come out and control themselves?"

"I don't want interference. Each alter does its part and stays there, protecting the whole system." My lips pressed together. "I'm sorry. I'm not cooperating."

"You're doing just fine," Margie reassured me. "At the same time, consider it. You need to be healed. I need to talk to them in a reasonable fashion. The walls need to come down."

I inhaled deeply. "They could lose their identity, disappear. Maybe I don't want that."

"You will know everybody, just like one happy family," Margie responded. "Why don't we start with a baby step. Would you be willing to put your fingers in your backyard pond and invite your alters to feel it with you? The water might feel cold. Share it. Enjoy it."

"I'm willing to give it a try," I said with a faint smile.

"How about imagining that you are at the end of a road that opens into a forest where you climb over a waterfall? You're on the top and look down. Oh, my! How beautiful, clear, wild. Can you see a glimpse, share it with others?"

I bit my lower lip. "No, I'm sorry. This is too much. I'm a mess."

"Ask God to put a hedge of protection around you. Only Jesus can set you free. Are you ready to talk about Jesus? I can't push you. I can't."

"I know that I believe in Jesus. He's protected me from my dark side. Given me the gift of dissociation. But the alters aren't here now. They can't hear you. It's just me, Sue."

Margie shook her head. "No, they are here, listening carefully."

"I don't think so."

"You know you have different personalities," Margie reminded me.

"I have no problems."

"But your personalities do. I know you have a good life, but I'd rather talk to the personalities."

I shrugged my shoulders, "They're not here."

Margie said, "They will come out if they want to."

After a few more minutes, our time was up. But in the following months of sessions, Margie continued to return to the topic of accepting my alters. By the time I reached my fourth year of counseling with Margie, I could see improvement. Some alters had begun to recognize their roles of protecting me. And that they weren't ugly, but just holding a lot of pain. Their attitude toward me softened with not so much hitting, hiding, or hateful remarks.

"I feel you're ready to move forward," Margie encouraged me. "To really work through your pain."

I shifted in my seat. "I do see a glimmer of hope. But there is still a part of me that likes to hit me over the head. I think I like to punish myself because I feel I deserve it."

"Experiencing physical pain is an immediate release," Margie pointed out. "The problem is that it allows you to avoid looking at the emotional pain that is pushing you to resort to physical punishment. We need to look at that underlying emotional pain."

My body rocked back and forth. "I'm afraid I'll have a breakdown like my father if I allow all those hidden memories and feelings to surface."

"That is why your alters believe they need to protect you," Margie explained. "But you need to trust me that you wouldn't have a breakdown now. Whatever the turmoil your alters experienced in the past, they are no longer in the same environment of fear, powerlessness, and helplessness. That's why they were there. But now you have support and are no longer at the mercy of your mother and father. Since you've grown emotionally and are now mature, you couldn't have a breakdown now."

"That all makes sense," I admitted. "But my dissociated parts are spooky, freaky, and abnormal. I'm not proud of them."

I knew Margie was right. I was not a little girl anymore. I also recognized how differently—and how much worse—my life might have turned out. What if I hadn't left my original junior high and met some new friends who supported me? What if I hadn't met my husband, who surrounded me with love and comfort? What if I hadn't come to know Jesus Christ as my Savior who loved me and protected me, including by giving me the gift of dissociation? I had so much to be grateful for.

Still, trying to understand my distorted, deranged, other selves reminded me uncomfortably of my own father and his mental illness. Once I arrived home, I dug out my copy of

Diagnostic and Statistical Manuel of Mental Health (DSM) and thumbed through its pages until I found one describing paranoia and schizophrenia as possible mental conditions that could be acted out in split personality. A paranoid personality disorder suspects without sufficient basis that others are harming or deceiving him or her. A schizophrenic can't distinguish what is real or imaginary. Yet the manual stated that these mental conditions were not caused from environmental factors. In my own case, there was no doubt my environment had contributed to displaced emotions too hard for me to endure as a child.

Putting down the manual, I went in search of my husband. Larry was reading a book in the family room, but looked up as I entered. I rushed into speech. "Larry, I know my alters are helping me, but I hate them. They are so weird. I try to be loveable. They are hateful. I'm peaceful. They're agitated. I'm normal. They're abnormal. I'm cheerful. They're angry. I could go on and on. I just wish they weren't there!"

"Why?" Larry responded calmly. "They're not hurting you. Didn't you say Dr. Marshall and Margie Alvarado have both said that you'd be in a sanitarium by now or would have committed suicide if they weren't carrying the pain for you and protecting you? You need to just accept them as your helpers."

"Then you don't mind if I continue going to therapy?" I asked.

"Not at all. I just want what's best for you."

"Thank you. I've really come to understand the intensity of my childhood abuse. And how my split personality has actually set me free to have a good life by carrying my trauma for me. I've also finally come to realize that my inner child has a voice that needs to be heard and loved. I need to listen to her and allow her to be a part of my everyday life."

"That's great!" Larry agreed heartily. "I've seen changes in you as well. You seem more relaxed. You're able to watch sports with me on television without jumping up to clean windows or washing the floor. And you can sit back on the outside chaise lounge without jumping up to pull weeds."

Larry added with a chuckle, "I've also noticed you have more of a temper. But that's okay. It's more normal than never showing anger and always being the positive, rational one."

I jumped up to give him a bear hug. "Oh Larry. Where were you the first seventeen years of my life?"

CHAPTER THIRTY-FOUR

TRUTH

And you shall know the truth and the truth well set you free.

—John 8:32

I continued counseling with Margie even when I reached the wise age of seventy-five, more than twenty years after I recognized I needed help to face the demons of my past. Thanks to God's gifts of patience and persistence, I've finally been able to face my inner child, my mother's neglect, the abuse from renters, the horrors of my father's insanity, the satanic oppression, and the raw feelings of fear and revulsion I'd kept buried for so many years.

Under Margie's skilled and compassionate treatment, the core of my disorder has seen healing. For the most part, my split personalities have been mollified. Many have integrated with me. Some have possibly kept their role as internal self-helpers for my safety and stabilization. That's okay. I've learned to not fight them. They were created to help me. We are a team.

These days I feel so good, so whole. I can show displeasure over ill treatment without fear of abandonment. I don't need constant approval and affirmation from others. I don't always have to be productive to feel worthwhile.

And I know God is on my side. He fights my battles. He set me free.

Among the many gifts from God for which I am deeply thankful is having both my daughters and their families living nearby. Dena and Donna know all about my counseling sessions and split personality, but they accept me as I am and remain my best friends. Dena, our oldest daughter, is married to Brandon, a computer programmer. They have two children, Zachary and Hannah. Our younger daughter Donna, is married to James, a lawyer. They have twins, Jack and Julia.

Both families are stable and loving. Through my grandchildren, I am now relishing vicariously the carefree joy of a childhood I myself never experienced. We chase each other around the house. We sprawl on the carpet with puzzles and board games. We pet the neighborhood horses and feed them carrots. My days end blissfully with wet kisses planted on my cheek.

I also rejoice in the continued fellowship of good friends whose positive role in my life goes back now for decades. Cleo remained one of my closest friends until she left this earth to step into glory. So did Louise, who'd first shared with me that God was my heavenly Father. Lyla remains my dearest friend and so do Linda, Charlene, and June.

Then there is my sister Sandy. We saw each other off-and-on through the years. But that she held a deep-rooted dislike for me, most likely caused from my mother's treatment of her, became increasingly apparent. When I could no longer ignore it, I called my sister, wanting to resolve the issue. But as we talked, my hurt emotions flew out of control. Afterward, I felt ashamed of my outburst and called her right back. But Sandy wouldn't accept my apology, saying I'd bothered her enough over the years. She hung up in my ear, and though I called her repeatedly over the next three years to apologize, she wouldn't talk to me.

Finally, I decided to just stop calling her. After all, why should I always be the nice one. Hadn't I grown beyond the stage of always having to please everyone? But no sooner had I made my decision when I could feel God's prompting on my heart to pick up the phone again.

"I can't!" I argued back. "She always yells at me. She won't talk to me."

I could sense God's response as clearly as though it were an audible voice. "Call her."

I called her. This time, she picked up the phone, and by the end of the conversation, we'd restored communication. A few weeks later, I saw Sandy at an Easter get-together. She was being distant again, and I was shocked at my own feelings of anger.

I don't like her! I told myself. A familiar guilt and confusion swept over me, and I found myself crying out to God, *Please, help me love my sister!* Walking over to Sandy, I gave her a hug.

"We're sisters!" I said to her. "I don't want us to quarrel."

At that moment, such a feeling of love for her swept over me. Looking up at me, Sandy returned my hug and said, "I'm sorry!"

Since then, our relationship has improved. Not long ago, when we were having lunch together, I asked, "Sandy, how did you manage to escape so well from our childhood trauma?"

Sandy folded and unfolded her napkin before responding, "I've learned from a young age to hide under a shell of protection and not let anyone see what's underneath, including myself. And not to trust anyone. Be independent. No expectations. Remember what Mother used to say. Don't trust anyone. Be independent. That's worked for me."

"So how do you feel about my altered selves?"

Sandy looked across at me. "I'm actually amazed. I feel a compassion for you, and I'm sorry I can't help you through it. At the same time, I don't feel sorry for you personally because of the good life you lead and your absolute control over these alters. I have a theory that we've had a curse on our family for a long time. You're the one to break it."

"Actually, it's interesting you say that," I responded. "I have these recurring, haunting images, maybe even memories, of a sorceress casting a curse on our family. In these memories, I see her in the desert, kneeling in the sand, wearing bright colors, head wrapped up in a turban, hands up toward the sky, chanting hexes and curses. The picture rings in my mind with enough force to knock me over. Where did it come from? How could it be in my imagination?"

"I have no idea," Sandy shrugged. "But if you think about it, our family is beset with problems. Alcoholism has been in our family for three generations. Daddy had severe mental breakdowns and committed suicide. His sister, Aunt Margaret, was just plain narcissistic. Aunt Ortha, had a nervous tic. Then there was our mother. There's so much we've never understood about her. She was plagued with her OCD and all those unreasonable fears like being afraid of magazines and fresh air and anything else that might give her germs."

"You're right," I agreed. "Her fears preoccupied her mind so much she had nothing left over to give to us."

My eyes watered. "We haven't brought up the horrible experiences of my own girls. Donna being assaulted by a Mexican policeman and her boyfriend trying to strangle her. Dena attempting suicide."

"Yes, you've had your own suffering and pain to face," Sandy agreed.

"Sandy, the Bible makes clear that a generational curse can only be broken by finding a new life in Jesus. It is coming to know Jesus as my Savior that has given me the assurance of His protection and redemption."

Sandy turned to head and stared out the window. "I don't like the mention of Jesus. In fact, I feel like I could break out in a sweat and dash out of here." She paused. "But I think you are meant to break the curse."

I haven't given up hope, and never will, that my sister will in time find the redemption, hope, and healing that I have found. In fact, I've already told Sandy point-blank that I will be preaching Christ to her till the last minute she draws breath.

As I parted from my sister and drove home, I mentally reviewed the very different coping mechanisms Sandy and I had developed to survive against overwhelming odds. She'd become anonymous, quiet, unobtrusive, learning to take care of herself and keep out of the way, wrapping herself up in a cocoon of protection against a world not to be trusted.

Conversely, I'd looked elsewhere for love, laughter, and acceptance. I'd been fortunate to find good friends who fulfilled my emotional needs through long telephone conversations, visiting each other's houses, going to parties, the beach, amusement centers. Then and now, my split personality has done an exceptional job, protecting me from pain and trauma, as well as keeping sealed my contradictory opposites from each other's view and my own.

I've continued working through my multiple personality disorder, no longer with any misgivings, but with thankfulness. As I've become more comfortable with my alters and their positive role in my life, I've also become less anxious about sharing my story and my condition with others. I now have a large support system of family and friends who know my story. Somewhat to my surprise, they haven't shown any signs of shock or horror. Instead, they have assured me of their friendship and their trust in me, the Sue Liston they've come to know over the years.

Their affirmation has encouraged me to share my story of childhood trauma, pain, and fractured self-identity, but also of God's protection, redemption, and bounteous blessings, with a far wider audience. In one of our sessions, I shared that desire with Margie.

"I'm surprised people who know my story don't run away, afraid of what I might do," I commented.

"So just why do you want to share your story?" she queried. "What do you feel your purpose is now?"

"To give people encouragement," I answered. "To help them recognize our adversary, the devil, and to walk toward the light that is in Jesus. God has been so good to me. He has lifted me up through problems that no one else could have solved. I want to help others who have felt rejected and rebuffed throughout life to turn to God and find the same joy and peace I have encountered."

"That sounds like a wonderful purpose," Margie responded, eyes moist. "Scripture tells us to comfort others with the same comfort we ourselves have received from God (2 Corinthians 1:4). I can't think of a better outcome to all you've been through. Go for it!"

And that is what I've done. Beginning with writing this book.

EPILOGUE

FUTURE HOPE

For I know the plans I have for you," declares the Lord, "plans to prosper you and not to harm you, plans to give you hope and a future.

—Jeremiah 29:11

So I come to the end of my story. After three-quarters of a century now on this earth, I am very much alive and well, far more so than in my childhood and youth. At seventy-five, I am still blessed with a sharp mind and a healthy body that I keep fit playing tennis, gardening, and other wholesome outdoor activities. I am blessed as well by close relationships with my family and many friends. Larry and I are both blessed to serve God actively in our church and to enjoy a full social life.

Yes, I have known pain. But God has wrought His purposes from my pain. He has turned the bad to good. He has always been with me in my times of need and in my dark places. Including sending me just the right counselors along the way.

Each of these counselors in turn —whether professional therapist, pastor, priest, missionary, psychologist—has played a vital role in my life right when I needed them most. They helped me recognize that my childhood family was dysfunctional, not me. That my feelings did not need to remain buried too deep to ever surface, but could be expressed when appropriate. Above all, that I am not crazy nor possessed of demons (though certainly I have endured demonic oppression), but victim of an actual mental condition—multiple personality disorder.

And along my long journey of self-discovery, I've also come to the wonderful assurance that my MPD and accompanying dissociation has not been a curse, a punishment, or even a disease, but a gift from God. Without that mental and emotional protection, I would likely have committed suicide or been institutionalized by now. God was and is watching out for me.

In the process of my journey, I've made peace with my multiple inner selves. To find healing for as many as ten different personalities, each frozen in time in a child's traumatized mind, has not been a short or easy process. It would not have been possible at all without Jesus as my guiding light. He is my ultimate Healer.

As I look back, I can see now that this story isn't just about God bringing me comfort and healing in the midst of pain. Because the pain itself can hold purpose. The painful parts of my life have not been a waste any more than the blessings I've been granted. My past hardships have given me empathy when dealing with other people's difficult life situations. They've helped me learn compassion and kindness.

My pain also led me to God. If I hadn't known pain, if my life had always run smooth, perhaps I'd never have been impelled to search God out until I came face to face with His grace, love and redemption. Or be where I am now, able to share my love of God, faith in Christ, and love of Scripture with others who are on their own journey of self-discovery and spiritual truth.

It's been six years of heart-searching, head-scratching, and burning the night oil since I first started writing this book under God's direction. As I reach the final page, it is my prayer that you, my reader, will take away from my experiences the same hope and healing that I have been granted. And that you might find encouragement that there are answers, no matter what the problem facing you.

We live in a world beset with problems. But our trials and tribulations and satanic snares are no match for God. And we have a Savior, Jesus Christ, who has overcome the world with all its tribulations (John 16:33). Remember the verse I shared with you clear back in the introduction of my story? Let me share it with you one more time:

> These things I have spoken to you, so that in Me [Jesus] you may have peace. In the world you have tribulation, but take courage; I[Jesus] have overcome the world
>
> —John 16:33

Our Creator, our Heavenly Father, designed us for glorious living and to worship and adore our Maker. He gives us strength and resilient spirits to endure. He gives us gifts to contribute in His beautiful tapestry of life.

So whatever your current situation in life, however dark and painful it might appear on the surface, be of good cheer. Take heart. Have courage. Because there is new life, fresh hope, and eternal healing available to you in the redeeming grace and power of our Lord and Savior Jesus Christ.

Choose life in Christ and live!

About the Author

Born in San Diego, Sue Liston graduated from San Diego State University with a teaching degree. She is a leader in Bible Study Fellowship. Married to a wonderful husband for more than fifty years, she has two daughters and four grandchildren whom she enjoys immensely. Along with teaching Bible studies and other volunteer work, Sue stays busy, happy, and healthy with her favorite hobbies of tennis, bridge, and gardening.

You can contact Sue at:

www.suelistonbks.com

Made in the USA
San Bernardino, CA
10 October 2017